# What People are Saying

"This is an important and well-documented piece of scholarship that greatly adds to our understanding of past and present church-state relations in America. Lillback's thoughtful and painstakingly detailed historical analysis documents where church-state myths and misconceptions come from and why they persist."

BYRON JOHNSON
Professor of Sociology
Co-Director, Institute for Studies of Religion
Director, Program on Prosocial Behavior
Baylor University

"Calling *Wall of Misconception* just a book is like calling Niagara just a waterfall. It is a powerful piece of intellectual ammunition in America's attempt to determine whether Judeo-Christian values are vital to her survival or whether they are obsolete relics obstructing progress toward a social utopia. The outcome could depend on how many people read this volume."

RABBI DANIEL LAPIN
Rabbinic Scholar and Author
Founding Rabbi, Pacific Jewish Center

"Secularists today would rewrite history and cause Americans to forget our strong religious heritage. It is vitally important that our rich religious background not be forgotten. Dr. Lillback is to be commended for his effort to insure that the importance of Judeo-Christian thought in the formation of our nation is remembered. This is an important book and a must-read."

JUDGE CHARLES W. PICKERING, SR.
Retired, US Fifth Circuit Court of Appeals

"Peter Lillback has done a magnificent job of marshaling the overwhelming documentary evidence that the American nation's civil governments rest squarely upon a Biblical foundation. While one might quarrel with some of Dr. Lillback's specific applications of that religious heritage, he leaves the open-minded reader with no doubt that the nation's claim of 'liberty and justice for all' will not endure if the secularists succeed in their effort to separate God from government. With the publication of this book, Dr. Lillback has furnished plenty of ammunition to win the battle that America was — and still is — 'one nation, under God.'"

HERBERT W. TITUS
Attorney-at-Law, William J. Olson, P.C.
Professor of Constitutional Law and former ACLU attorney
Founding Dean, College of Law and Government, Regent University (1986-1993)

"There is mounting evidence that most of the early American republic's key leaders were far closer to holding traditional Judeo-Christian beliefs and tenets than they were to harboring any strictly secular worldviews. Peter A. Lillback explores this evidence and relates it to present-day, church-state cases and controversies. Agree or disagree with Lillback's conclusions, *Wall of Misconception* makes for fascinating and informative reading. This book extends his justly influential writing on George Washington's religious identity, and challenges materialists to come reason together with thinking, orthodox believers."

JOHN J. DIIULIO, JR.
Founding Director, White House Office of Faith-Based and Community Initiatives
Professor of Political Science, University of Pennsylvania

# Wall *of* Misconception

# Wall *of* Misconception

DOES THE SEPARATION OF CHURCH
AND STATE MEAN THE SEPARATION
OF GOD AND GOVERNMENT?

# PETER A. LILLBACK

*Bestselling Author of "George Washington's Sacred Fire"*

PROVIDENCE FORUM PRESS

Wall of Misconception
Copyright © 2007 by Peter Lillback. All rights reserved.

ISBN: 0-9786052-3-3
ISBN13: 978-0-9786052-3-0

*Unless otherwise indicated, all scripture references are from the King James version of the Bible (KJV).*

Cover and Interior Design by Roark Creative: www.roarkcreative.com

All illustrations included are used by permission. Detailed credit list is included in the Endnotes.

For Library of Congress Control Number, please contact the publisher.

Printed in the United States of America by Hamilton Printing Company
2008—First Edition


Providence Forum Press
The Providence Forum
One Tower Bridge
100 Front Street, Suite 1415
West Conshohocken, Pennsylvania 19428
www.providenceforum.org

# Dedication

To all the pastors worldwide, whether enjoying freedom or enduring
persecution, who, according to their consciences, seek to speak
the truth in love.

# Contents

# Acknowledgements

I wish to thank all who have helped make this book a reality. As always, I thank God for my family and my friends who have stood with me as we have sought to produce a study that is accessible and engaging for Americans.

First, I thank the Board and Staff of The Providence Forum and the Elders and Staff of Proclamation Presbyterian Church for their gracious assistance and encouragement that has enabled the printing of this book. Second, I express my gratitude to all at Coral Ridge Ministries who wanted to see this book shared broadly with the nation. Third, I wish to express my deep respect for the labors of Francis Schaeffer, since his seminal works on the Christian worldview and the role of Christianity in the public square are what first prompted me to consider these questions. I offer my gratitude to all of the professionals who have prepared this text for publication—without their diligence, artistry, and wisdom, *The Wall of Misconception* would never have seen the light of day. Lastly, I express my deep respect for the three County Commissioners of Chester County, Pennsylvania who chose to stand boldly for the continuing witness of the historic Judeo-Christian value system in public life that ultimately prompted the writing of this book.

Thank you, dear reader, for taking the time to consider these questions that will greatly impact our nation's future and the destiny of religious liberty in America.

# Foreword

## by U.S. Senator Rick Santorum

In 2002, Michael Newdow, an atheist lawyer with a daughter in a California public school, challenged the constitutionality of the Pledge of Allegiance. Newdow argued that although his daughter was not required to recite the pledge, she was injured "when compelled to watch and listen as her state-employed teacher in her state-run school led her classmates in a ritual proclaiming that there is a God and that ours is 'one nation under God.'" A federal Ninth Circuit appellate panel agreed with Newdow, ruling that the words "under God" constituted an establishment of religion and hence, violated the First Amendment. Despite popular outrage and bi-partisan criticism of the decision in Congress, a second Ninth Circuit panel reaffirmed the original ruling in early 2003, again declaring the Pledge of Allegiance unconstitutional.

The American people were overwhelmingly surprised and outraged at the ruling, as well they should have been. However, the uncomfortable truth is that the Ninth Circuit's decision declaring the Pledge of Allegiance unconstitutional has a certain perverse logic, given the Supreme Court's confused church-state jurisprudence over the past half-century. The decision of the Ninth Circuit simply confirmed what conservative critics of the Supreme Court have been saying for decades, namely that so-called "strict separationist" interpretations of the First Amendment's "Establishment Clause" based on the "wall of separation" metaphor is not merely neutral toward religion, but hostile toward religious sentiment and results in driving religion out of the public square. Despite their protestations, this is the direct result of the influence of "strict separationist" advocacy organizations such as the American Civil Liberties Union, Americans United for the Separation of Church and State, and People for the American Way.

The First Amendment to the U.S. Constitution begins, "Congress shall make no law respecting the establishment of religion, or prohibiting the free exercise thereof...." For over the past half-century, a small but influential cadre of academics, activists, and activist judges has tried to insist that the First Amendment's "no Establishment Clause" requires a "high wall of separation of church and state." For decades these activists and jurists sought to defend this view as an accurate description of the views of the founders generally, and that it expressed the intent of the authors of the First Amendment. Their favorite citation was Thomas Jefferson's private letter to the Danbury Baptists in which he referred to a "wall of separation" between church and state.

However, as Dr. Lillback shows, as a simple historical matter, our founders were more than willing to accommodate religious expression and symbols in the public square. Indeed, in word and deed they encouraged it. That is why Justice William Rehnquist was right to declare over two decades ago in his Dissenting Opinion in *Wallace v. Jaffree* (1985), that, "The 'wall of separation between church and state' is a metaphor based on bad history, a metaphor which has proved useless as a guide to judging. It should be frankly and explicitly abandoned."

Justice Rehnquist was probably being too charitable. Not only has the "wall of separation metaphor" been useless, it is often more incoherent and pernicious than that. One here recalls the famous quip of Senator Daniel Patrick Moynihan remarking on the massive confusion generated by a series of Supreme Court decisions which ruled that while a state could permissibly lend school books to parochial schools without violating the Establishment Clause, it was unconstitutional to lend teaching aids and maps. That caused Senator Moynihan to ask about the constitutionality of an atlas, a book of maps.

Senator Moynihan's caustic quip was a pithy way of saying that a consistent application of the high wall of separation principle leads to absurd results. As one informed commentator observed,

> The Pledge case reveals that something has gone drastically wrong with Establishment Clause jurisprudence. If the Pledge is unconstitutional, so too are teacher-led recitations of the Gettysburg Address. Lincoln claimed "that this nation, under God, shall have a new birth of freedom." Teaching public school students that the Declaration of

Independence is true—that our rights are, in fact, "endowed by our Creator" and that the American Revolution was just according to the "Laws of Nature and of Nature's God"—would violate the Constitution. Even an invited performer signing "God Bless America" at a government-sponsored event, like a local county fair, would be constitutionally suspect. ("Establishing Free Exercise" by Vincent Phillip Muñoz in *First Things*, December 2003)

When the Declaration of Independence can in some light be thought constitutionally suspect, and would be but for public outcry at a judicially-imposed decision, it is long past time to reexamine the basis for the precedents that lead to such absurdities.

The fundamental problem, of course, is not simply the bad history and the absurdities that would result from a consistent application of the "high wall of separation" principle. The fundamental problem, as Dr. Lillback suggests, are activist judges willing to impose their own ideological understanding of the proper relation between religion and public life. Typically, such an understanding is based on the highly controversial opinion that religion is a purely private affair, that religiously informed argument in the public square is at best a barrier to enlightened discourse and at worst sows the seeds of intolerance and bigotry.

The consequences of this view go well beyond the impact on individuals' and groups' rights to freedom of expression and religion, they cut to the heart of what is required to sustain our democracy. This grand experiment is not guaranteed to last forever, and our founders understood the necessity of the electorate to be a virtuous people for freedom to be maintained, and that religion is essential to form virtue. A diminished or ghettoized civic religion will only diminish our democracy and threaten its sustainability.

Here we must be clear. If the American people, for whatever reason, through their elected representatives decide that the Ten Commandments should be removed from local court houses, that "under God" should be removed from the Pledge of Allegiance, that "In God We Trust" be removed from currency and coinage, that legislative and military chaplains should no longer be paid out of public funds, that Christmas nativity scenes should be removed from areas of public display, or that the Supreme Court should no longer open with a declaration of "God save this honorable court," then it is perfectly in keeping with the Constitution and the democratically determined decisions of a free people to do so. While I do not think such decisions would be wise, the Constitution does not require the presence of such symbols. It does, however, permit them, and activist judges exceed their authority when they require their removal, and they deserve derision when the try to persuade us that support for such can be found in either the text of the Constitution, in the meaning or intent of the authors, the history of the American republic. And if confused Establishment Clause precedents logically lead to such absurd and pernicious results, then it is long past time to reconsider those precedents.

U.S. Senator Rick Santorum

*Rick Santorum served as U.S. senator from Pennsylvania from 1995 to 2007 and as a member of the U.S. House of Representatives from 1991 to 1995. He is a senior fellow at the Ethics and Public Policy Center in Washington, D.C., a consultant with the law firm Eckert Seamans Cherin & Mellott LLC, and a contributor to the Fox News Channel.*

# *the* Article

The following is an article I wrote,
published by The Providence Forum in the fall of 2002:

## September 11th and the 9th Circuit Court:
## At Least For the Moment,
## We are still "One Nation Under God"

When the Ninth Circuit Court declared that the Pledge of Allegiance
was unconstitutional, many finally began to understand. In spite of all our
national expression of dependence on God in the aftermath of September
11th, there is still a relentless movement afoot to strip our nation's Judeo-
Christian heritage from our official culture. Its message is, "Sure, in the privacy
of your home, say the Pledge, but don't force your belief in God down the
throats of the rest of our secular nation!"

While this decision made the headlines of our national news, a more quiet,
but just as potent assault was occurring in the federal courthouse in
Philadelphia. The verdict reached by a single judge, without a jury of the
people, in less than twenty four hours, was that the Ten Commandments that
had been on the wall of Chester County's Courthouse, had to come down.
Once again, the theme was, "To have such statements in public is to violate the
First Amendment by making our secular nation acknowledge God." It was
ironic, indeed, that the same court opened with the declaration "God save the
Court of the United States!" We must be clear. This movement will not stop
if they are successful here. God in government is the enemy. Nothing less than
his utter and total removal from public discourse is the goal.

"For such a time as this," The Providence Forum has been called into
being. Our existence through your support has enabled us boldly to remind our
culture in federal courtrooms, on courthouse steps, at Independence Hall, in

17

academic institutions, in the presence of the president himself, that our Judeo-Christian heritage gave birth to this great nation of religious and civil liberty.

In spite of our nation's spiritual interest expressed recently in the memorial services on the first anniversary of the terrorists' attacks, the day may come when we are forced to censor even the Declaration of Independence and the Constitution. But let us until then not fail to declare that the first teaches us of "our Creator," of "the God of nature," of "the supreme Judge of the world," and the "protection of Divine Providence," and the later was written in "the year of our LORD, 1787." May our Lord graciously use all of our efforts to preserve and advance this legacy of liberty bequeathed to us by our founders.

Perhaps in the wake of news stories such as ominous potential terrorist attacks, the homosexual abuse of boys by priests, the malfeasance of auditing firms in league with deceiving corporate entities, and the violent volatility of the financial markets, we may once again wish to be "one nation under God" after all!

By the way, a good reason to get registered and to vote is that our elected officials appoint our federal judges. Your vote indirectly elects judges who either believe or do not believe that we are "one nation under God."

Dr. Peter A. Lillback

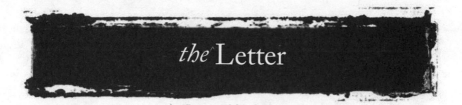

*the* Letter

This is the letter written to me by a pastor who had read the preceding article, and was thereby prompted to write the following:

Dear Dr. Lillback,

I enjoyed reading the latest issue of the Providence Forum's newsletter. Thank you for sending it. I also appreciate – and share – your mission: "to promote the Judeo-Christian worldview within our culture." I hope that God grants you success in your endeavors.

However, I can not, for the life of me, understand why anyone would fail to see the problem with requiring public school students to recite their allegiance to "one nation under God." Likewise, I have trouble understanding why there was an uproar over the decision to remove the Ten Commandments plaque from the Chester County Courthouse.

I see two problems with this blending of church and state:

- Those who are not Jewish or Christian should not have to pay homage to a creed that is not their own. Neither should they have to support our mission with their tax dollars.
- In order for the government to support Judeo-Christian values without trampling on the rights of non-Jews and non-Christians, those values have to be watered down to the point that they have very little to do with the gospel of Jesus Christ.

There are many avenues available to us Christians for promoting our worldview. We do not need to harness the government into doing it for us.

Please don't take this letter as a protest. Rather, I am sincerely seeking answers from an organization that might be able to provide them.

Sincerely,

Pastoral Associate

# *the* Response

The text that follows is largely the response I wrote to the pastor upon receiving the previous letter. However, for this book, additional material has been added. This includes a discussion of George Washington's presidential precedents; the augmentation of the history of the creation of the First Amendment; and the inclusion of the worldview charts and the appendices. The text and outline of the book, however, are essentially the response to the questions and issues raised by the letter that the pastor sent to me.

It should also be noted that the Chester County Court House Ten Commandments case, that was so hurriedly decided, as mentioned in the herein reprinted article, was unanimously overturned by the Third Circuit Court on appeal. So the plaque remains in place, thanks to the courage of the Chester County Pennsylvania Commissioners, who persevered in their commitment to preserve our Judeo-Christian historical presence in the public square.

# chapter 1

# GOD IN THE PUBLIC SQUARE

## PUBLIC SCHOOLS AND THE PLEDGE OF ALLEGIANCE.

"However, I cannot, for the life of me, understand why anyone would fail to see the problem with requiring public school students to recite their allegiance to 'one nation under God.'"

Your comment clearly raises the question of the legitimacy of using the Pledge of Allegiance in public settings. We might ask, "Can official 'secular' documents make reference to God"? Ultimately, your question raises the matter of which worldview will impact our national thinking.

*President Dwight D. Eisenhower – "We are reaffirming the transcendence of religious faith in America's heritage and future."*

Your candid astonishment that "anyone" could miss the "problem" of requiring public school students to recite their allegiance to "one nation under God" is peculiar indeed. Long before your letter was written—about a half-century ago—Congress passed the act that incorporated the words "under God" into the pledge. At that time, President Dwight D. Eisenhower, along with the United States Congress, perceived a very different problem facing America than the one you fear. It was to find a national point of transcendence that would enable America to remain strong in the face of daunting challenges to the very fabric of American freedom.

## The Historical Context of the Pledge of Allegiance

You are undoubtedly aware of the history of the Pledge. However, many Americans do not know that the phrase "under God" was not in the original form when it was written by Francis Bellamy, a Baptist minister from Boston in 1892, which was the four-hundredth anniversary of Columbus' discovery of America. Sixty-two years later, on Flag Day, June 14, 1954, President Eisenhower signed the legislation that added "under God" to the Pledge. Explaining his support for Congressional Act, Joint Resolution 243, he declared,

> In this way we are reaffirming the transcendence of religious faith in America's heritage and future; in this way we shall constantly strengthen those spiritual weapons which forever will be our country's most powerful resource in peace and war.

These words are particularly significant coming from President

Eisenhower. Only a decade before, he had been the military commander of the most powerful force ever assembled in history. Yet in his view, the most powerful weapons for our nation in peace or in war were not economic or military, but spiritual. In his mind, the government had nothing to fear from faith, for America's government understood the importance of faith in the nation's past and its need for such trust in its future.

In fact, the Pledge's new language of "under God" had its source in Lincoln's immortal Gettysburg Address. Lincoln believed that the healing of a nation torn asunder by civil war and grieving in the face of the unparalleled human carnage of the Gettysburg battlefield could only be found when the afflicted nation saw its proper place as being "under God." Thus, in the Gettysburg Address, delivered on November 19, 1863, "the theologian of American anguish" encouraged his fellow citizens affirming,

> It is rather for us to be here dedicated to the great task remaining before us—that from these honored dead we take increased devotion to that cause for which they gave the last full measure of devotion—

*President Abraham Lincoln at Gettysburg – "This nation, under God, shall have a new birth of freedom."*

that we here highly resolve that these dead shall not
have died in vain that this nation, under God, shall
have a new birth of freedom—and that government
of the people, by the people, for the people, shall not
perish from the earth.

Given this history, background, and sources, it is no wonder that school
children and adult teachers used to say daily the Pledge of Allegiance. Perhaps
you can remember saying it yourself.

Yet you are concerned that children might be "required" to pledge
allegiance to a flag that represents "one nation under God." Clearly, we must
be concerned about protecting the religious liberty of our students, but is it
possible that this liberty of conscience exists precisely because historically we
have claimed to be a "nation under God"?

## Recent Cultural and Constitutional Viewpoints Impacting the Use of the Pledge of Allegiance

What has transpired in the half century between President Eisenhower's
enacting the words "under God" into the pledge and into law in 1954 and the
opposing view of the U. S. Ninth Circuit Court's 2002 ruling that holds that
the use of the pledge is unconstitutional? To answer this, we must come to
grips with the massive shift of worldviews and cultural values that has occurred
in the past half century.

An incredible sea change has in fact occurred in public opinion, worldview,
and governmental policy in these last decades. Actually, to better understand
this, a good place to start is by considering your own words as a pastor
expressing his concerns about what he sees as God's role in the public square.

Initially, notice the assumption that is made by your statement "requiring
to recite their allegiance." The fact is that no one in America is "required" to
say the pledge! Free speech is our First Amendment constitutional
heritage. The very way you have couched the matter masks what is really
transpiring in the Court's decision. Today, we are encouraged and permitted
to recite our allegiance to the flag by using the words "one nation under God."
Should we choose to do so, we are doing it in a lawful way. Should we choose
*not* to say it, we are doing so in a constitutional way. Where is the reality
of "required" action in this discussion? It is in the Ninth Circuit

Court's move to strike the 1954 Congressional Act, Joint Resolution 243 as unconstitutional!

While the Supreme Court's decision not to review this decision leaves the pledge in force in all areas except the Ninth Circuit, if that ruling were ultimately to become the opinion of the Supreme Court, we would be "required" to forego saying the pledge ever again in a public setting. What then becomes of our free speech? What then becomes of religious liberty for those who can in good conscience say the pledge in its legal form? They will no longer be encouraged and permitted to do so. They will be required not to recite their allegiance.

Isn't it interesting that you have unconsciously misstated the entire matter? By allowing our rhetoric to be controlled by inaccurate terminology, we are not only going to lose our historic freedom to say or not to say the pledge, but we will have unconsciously abandoned a freedom for a court mandated lawful behavior. Sadly, we will never even know what hit us. This process of the erosion of our liberties was well understood by the great architect of our Constitution, James Madison, when he said,

> Since the general civilization of mankind, I believe there are more instances of the abridgment of the freedom of the people, by gradual and silent encroachments of those in power, than by violent and sudden usurpations. (James Madison, Virginia Convention, June 6, 1788. In Padover, *The Complete Madison*, 339)

## Worldviews in Collision: Competing Answers to Ultimate Questions

Christian cultural analyst, the late Francis Schaeffer, agreed with Madison's insight. Schaeffer argued that our culture's movements away from Christianity's values are the consequence of a conscious shift in how people interpret their world.

> The basic problem of the Christians in this country... in regard to society and in regard to government, is that they have seen things in bits and pieces instead of totals. They have very gradually

become disturbed over permissiveness, pornography, the public schools, the breakdown of the family, and finally abortion. But they have not seen this as a totality – each thing being a part, a symptom, of a much larger problem. They have failed to see that all of this has come about due to a shift in worldview–that is, through a fundamental change in the overall way people think and view the world and life as a whole. This shift has been away from a worldview that was at least vaguely Christian in people's memory toward something completely different... (Francis A. Schaeffer, *A Christian Manifesto*, Crossway Books, 1981, 17-18)

So worldviews clearly matter. So, how should we define worldview? Actually, as you likely know, the term worldview is a word that comes to us from the German equivalent, *Weltanschauung*. In 1933, in a lecture called "The Question of a Weltanschauung," the world famous atheist, psychologist, and philosopher Sigmund Freud defined a worldview as "an intellectual construction, which solves all the problems of our existence uniformly on the basis of one overriding hypothesis." The point is that if we are to address the ultimate questions of life, we are inevitably led to a concern to construct a worldview.

We all have wondered about our lives with the powerful words of who, what, why....? These questions are found everywhere—in the curiosity of children, the contemplations of philosophers, and in our deepest inner-life. The inner struggles that are evoked by these questions, we either seek to resolve or we strive to ignore or suppress. Dr. Armand Nicholi, associate clinical professor of psychiatry at Harvard Medical School, explained it this way:

All of us, whether we realize it or not, have a worldview; we have a philosophy of life—our attempt to make sense out of our existence. It contains our answers to the fundamental questions concerning the meaning of our lives, questions that

we struggle with at some level all of our lives, and
that we often think about only when we wake up at
three o'clock in the morning. The rest of the time
when we are alone we have the radio or the
television on—anything to avoid being alone with
ourselves. Pascal maintained the sole reason for our
unhappiness is that we are unable to sit alone in our
room. He claimed we do not like to confront the
reality of our lives; the human condition is so
basically unhappy that we do everything to keep
distracted from thinking about it." (*The Real Issue*,
vol. 16, number 2, January 1997, 9)

Every worldview consciously or unconsciously seeks to answer the
ultimate questions about our lives. Who am I? Why am I here? Do I have a
soul? Is man free? What is wrong with the world? Is there a God? Has he
spoken? Is there a true religion? Is there life after death? And there are many
more of these worldview questions. Our worldview is our explanation of these
great questions.

But the radical issue of our hypotheses of life or worldview that answers
these ultimate questions of human existence is simply this: Our lives are the
experiment that tests our hypothesis! What if the experiment fails, and we
discover that our hypothesis was false? Then what? Our life is over.
Determining one's answers to the ultimate questions implicit in worldview
consideration has ultimate consequences.

Throughout history, Christianity has given answers to these questions.
These answers explain the impact the Judeo-Christian heritage has had on
human cultures. Consider a few examples of social change provided by
Christianity.

In the Roman Empire in the early years of the Christian Era:

Many permanent legal reforms were set in motion
by Emperors Constantine (280-337) and Justinian
(483-565) that can be laid to the influence of
Christianity. Licentious and cruel sports were
checked; new legislation was ordered to protect the

slave, the prisoner, the mutilated man, and the outcast woman. Children were granted important legal rights. Women were raised from a status of degradation to that of legal protection. Hospitals and orphanages were created to take care of foundlings. Personal feuds and private wars were put under restraint. Branding of slaves was halted. (Sherwood Wirt, *The Social Conscience of the Evangelical*, Harper and Row, 1967, 31)

In the Medieval Era the value of human life became normative as the Christian worldview sought to create order in the collapse of the Roman Empire:

Before the explosive and penetrating growth of medieval Christian influence, the primordial evils of abortion, infanticide, abandonment and exposure were a normal part of everyday life in Europe. Afterward, they were regarded as the grotesque perversions that they actually are. That remarkable new pro-life consensus was detonated by a cultural reformation of cosmic proportions. It was catalyzed by civil decrees, ecclesiastical canons, and merciful activity. (George Grant, *Third Time Around: A History of the Pro-Life Movement from the First Century to the Present*, Legacy Publishing Company, 1991, 20)

This is also seen in the era of the founding of America. America's western civilization was an outgrowth of the Reformation era. The Protestant ideal of biblical wisdom seen in its teaching of "Sola Scriptura" helped to create our institutions of government:

Over a ten-year period, political science professors at the university of Houston analyzed over 15,000 writings and speeches by the Founding Fathers to determine the primary source of ideas behind the Constitution. The three most quoted sources were the French philosopher Charles Montesquieu, English jurist William Blackstone, and English philosopher John Locke. But the Bible was quoted more than any of these: four times more than Montesquieu, six times more often than Locke, and twelve times more than Blackstone. Ninety-four percent of the Founding Fathers' quotes were quoted, either directly or indirectly, from the Bible. (David T. Moore, *Five Lives of the Century*, Tyndale House Publishers, 1995, 9-10)

It is therefore of immense importance to men to have fixed ideas about God, their soul, and their duties toward their Creator and their fellows, for doubt about these first principles would leave all their actions to chance and condemn them, more or less, to anarchy and impotence. (Alexis de Toqueville, *Democracy in America*, 1838)

As Gary DeMar has written: *"It's the power of regeneration, not revolution, that brings about change to individuals who then reform families, churches, businesses, and every other feature of God's kingdom."* (From: *War of the Worldviews*)

But there has been a major shift away from Christianity in the prevailing worldviews of the mid-twentieth century that continues to directly impact us today. In 1909, President Theodore Roosevelt said, regarding a "Christian Civilization":

Progress has brought us both unbounded opportunities and unbridled difficulties. Thus, the measure of our civilization will not be that we have done much, but what we have done with that much. I believe that the next half-century will determine if we will advance the cause of Christian civilization or revert to the horrors of brutal paganism. The thought of modern industry in the hands of Christian charity is a dream worth dreaming. The thought of industry in the hands of paganism is a nightmare beyond imagining. The choice between the two is upon us.*

*President Theodore Roosevelt – "The next half-century will determine if we will advance the cause of Christian civilization or revert to the horrors of brutal paganism."*

Roosevelt's half century brought America to 1959. In 1962-63, the Bible and prayer were banished from America's schools. In 1973, abortion on demand was legalized as the indispensable corollary of the sexual revolution. If America ever was a "Christian nation," after 1970, it certainly would be one no longer—American government must be secular, and religion must be exclusively a private matter. In the 1980s the Ten Commandments, along with other evidences of America's historical interest in Christianity, were stripped from the walls of public buildings. In the early 1990s, our culture was inundated by the issues of gay-rights and euthanasia. Roosevelt's prescience is astonishing.

New Age mystic Marilyn Ferguson analyzed the impact of the sixties with chilling accuracy. Said Ferguson, "The values that had powered the movement of the sixties could not be institutionalized without a shift in cultural assumptions. As consciousness changes, the world changes."* The change has occurred. Americans not only tolerate but have institutionalized divorce, abortion, homosexuality, and feminism. This has happened because the religious consciousness of America has changed. (Peter Jones, *Spirit Wars: Pagan Revival in America*, Wine Press Publishing, 1997, 15-16) No wonder there are so many who no longer want to say "one nation under God"!

What should those who embrace the historic Judeo-Christian worldview do about this worldview shift that is so impacting our culture? Dr. Armand Nicholi notes: "There are several things one can do to better integrate his or her worldview, including developing a distinct, vocational philosophy, developing a biblical theology, and discovering the structure of your discipline."

(Dr. Armand Nicholi, *The Real Issue*, vol. 16, number 2, January 1997, 9)

Since the influence of secularism is so great, we need to appreciate how secular worldviews differ from the historic Judeo-Christian worldview of our founders and the earlier American culture.

## Secularism: Humanism and Materialism— The Impersonal Universe of the Blind Clockmaker

One of the most powerful worldview perspectives to challenge the Judeo-Christian worldview is what has been called secularism. Secularists take many philosophical forms. They are sometimes identified as humanists or materialists. Understandably, the secular humanists or materialists want to impact the world with their worldview. The agenda of secularism is largely atheistic in nature. Thus, humanism has the notion of man's absolute independence from God. John Whitehead in his work *The Second American Revolution* writes:

> For our present purposes, humanism can be defined as the fundamental idea that men and women can begin from themselves without reference to the Bible and, by reasoning outward, derive the standards to judge all matters. For such people, there are no absolute or fixed standards of behavior. They are quire literally autonomous (from the Greek *autos*, self, and *nomos*, law), a law unto themselves. There are no rights given by God. There are no standards that cannot be eroded or replaced by what seems necessary, expedient, or even fashionable at the time. Man is his own authority, "his own god in his own universe." (p. 38)

While it is beyond the scope of my plan here to provide a survey of the history of secularism in America, we do need to understand a few basic ideas. To get started, let's summarize a few important ideas. As you know, historic Judeo-Christian thought holds to a worldview marked by seven key ideas: God, Revelation, Creation, the Fall, Redemption, God's Will, and Hope.

| KEY IDEAS | THE CHRISTIAN VIEW | IMPLICATIONS |
|---|---|---|
| **Ultimate Reality** | GOD<br>Eternal / personal | This view is called theism. God is personal. |
| **The Source of Truth** ("How do we know?") | REVELATION<br>General and Special | General revelation is in nature. Special revelation is in scripture and in Christ. |
| **The Origins of All Things** | CREATION<br>Man has dignity.<br>There is order/ purpose/meaning. | Nature is God's handiwork, so all truth is God's truth. Science thinks God's thoughts after him. |
| **Death / Evil** | FALL<br>The judgment of God produces human suffering and death. | Nature is not "normal"; it is broken and hurting in a fallen world. |
| **The Improvement of the Human Condition** | "Summum bonum" or highest good is REDEMPTION, salvation and the kingdom of God both in the "here and now" and "there and then" | Man cannot remedy his deepest need from within. He is in need of grace from without—from the love of God in salvation. |
| **Ethics** | GOD'S WILL<br>In the Ten Commandments and scripture are our standards. We have absolute values. | Man does not do what is right in his own eyes. He is to live in obedience to the wisdom and will of God. |
| **The Ultimate Destiny of Man and the Universe** | HOPE<br>Resurrection – Restoration<br>Heaven or Hell | There is life after death. There is final justice. There is hope in the mercy of God. |

The Christian worldview holds to the concept of knowledge by revelation. *(See Chart 1)*

## CHART 1

## The Theism of Biblical Christianity: Truth by Divine Revelation

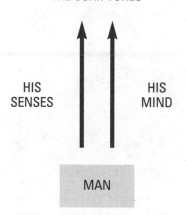

**GOD AND TRUTH**
There is a supernatural realm.
It can be known because of God's
self-disclosure.

**DIVINE REVELATION**

The Limits of Nature and Human Knowledge

THE SCRIPTURES

HIS
SENSES

HIS
MIND

MAN

But as theological liberalism impacted Christian thought in the wake of the European enlightenment, there was a loss of faith in the scriptures as God's self-revelation. With the rejection of revelation, Protestant liberal theology adopted the deist model of a God who does not speak to mankind in scripture. *(See Chart #2)*

# CHART 2

## Deism and Protestant Liberalism

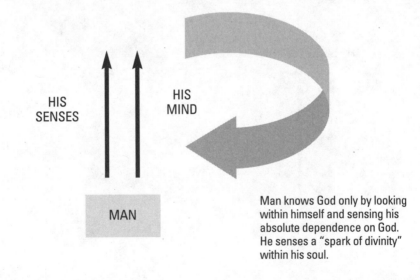

**GOD AND TRUTH**
There is a supernatural realm,
but it cannot be known.

The Limits of Nature and Human Knowledge
There is no Divine Revelation in the Scriptures

HIS
SENSES

HIS
MIND

MAN

Man knows God only by looking
within himself and sensing his
absolute dependence on God.
He senses a "spark of divinity"
within his soul.

This rejection of revelation has led many to reject the notion of God altogether. This atheistic viewpoint is at the core of the secularists' view of God and all human knowledge. *(See Chart #3)*

CHART 3

Secular Materialism

NO GOD
THERE IS NOTHING BUT MATTER
No supernatural realm beyond nature.

The Limits of Nature and Human Knowledge

Man exists entirely in a materialistic
universe. He is autonomous—
a law to himself.

By his senses and his reason alone
he interprets nature and his life.

This atheistic worldview is held by systems such as
humanism, materialism, nihilism, existentialism, communism

Ultimately, the worldview of the Judeo-Christian and that of the secularist are at polar opposites. Consider this next chart.

## A COMPARISON OF CHRISTIANITY AND SECULAR MATERIALISM:

# The Foundational Concepts of Two of the Dominant Competing Contemporary Worldviews

| VIEW OF | CHRISTIAN | MATERIALIST |
|---|---|---|
| **Ultimate Reality** | GOD<br>Eternal / personal | matter / energy<br>eternal / impersonal |
| **The Source of Truth**<br>("How do we know?") | REVELATION<br>General and Special | autonomous reason and experience |
| **The Origins of All Things** | CREATION<br>dignity, order<br>purpose/meaning | CHAOS/TIME/CHANCE<br>no "unalienable rights"<br>or eternal significance<br>We create our purpose. |
| **Death / Evil** | FALL<br>The judgment of God<br>produces human suffering<br>and death. | MINDLESS NATURAL FORCES:<br>Random and purposeless<br>suffering |
| **The Improvement of the Human Condition** | "Summum bonum" or<br>highest good is<br>REDEMPTION, salvation<br>and the kingdom of<br>God both in the "here<br>and now" and "there<br>and then" | "Summum bonum" or highest<br>good is man's solution of<br>SELF-ACTUALIZATION,<br>education, and social service;<br>"here and now," not "there<br>and then." |
| **Ethics** | GOD'S WILL<br>In the Ten Commandments<br>and scripture are our<br>standards. We have<br>absolute values. | MAN'S WILL<br>Establishes standards for life.<br>No absolutes; all is relative.<br>"Every man does what<br>is right in his own eyes."<br>Post-modernity's<br>expressive individualism. |
| **The Ultimate Destiny of Man and the Universe** | HOPE<br>Resurrection –<br>Restoration<br>Heaven or Hell | DESPAIR<br>Extinction and oblivion of<br>humanity in the repetition<br>of the endless cycle of the<br>explosion and contraction<br>of the universe...or the eternal<br>freezing of all matter and<br>energy in the final state of<br>thermodynamic equilibrium |

I think you can see why I believe there has been a huge sea change in the way people look at the world today. That clearly impacts how we understand the notion of "one nation under God" affirmed in the classic language of the Pledge of Allegiance.

# chapter 2

# THE PLEDGE OF ALLEGIANCE AT THE INTERSECTION OF WORLDVIEWS

"However, I cannot, for the life of me, understand why anyone would fail to see the problem with requiring public school students to recite their allegiance to 'one nation under God.'"

Your comment also raises the question of the value of using the Pledge of Allegiance in public settings to safeguard the liberties that we as Americans have enjoyed for so long.

I believe that the use of the pledge in our schools is actually an important tool to prevent the erosion of our liberties. To quote James Madison,

"Learned institutions ought to be favorite objects with every free people. They throw that light over the public mind which is the best security against crafty and dangerous encroachments on the public liberty." (To W. T. Barry, August 4, 1822. In *The Complete Madison: His Basic Writings*, ed. Saul K. Padover, [New York: Harper & Brothers, 1953], 337)

Thus, I believe that liberty is lost, not gained, by the court-imposed limitation of First Amendment free speech in the required silence, with respect to the public use of the pledge. Stripping America's historic and legal use of the pledge is, in my mind, what Madison meant by "crafty and dangerous encroachments on the public liberty."

I believe that you are also making a further assumption that somehow one of the words or one of the combination of the words "public," or "school," or "students" is somehow inconsistent with reciting one's "allegiance to 'one nation under God.'" I believe this is an erroneous assumption. My guess is that you do not have problems with any "public school" or any "public school students" pledging allegiance to the "oneness" of the nation or to the "nation" itself. I would also suspect that you would have no real problem with "school students" pledging their allegiance to "one nation under God," so long as the school and the students were private or parochial or religious. Your real problem is the concatenation of "public" as an adjective of "school" and/or "children" with the phrase "under God." The reason for that is because you assume that "under God" is inherently "religious" while the word "public" necessarily pertains to government, which by modern renditions of the First Amendment must be kept strictly neutral, i.e., the separation of church ("under God") and state ("public").

This perspective is widely received as undisputedly authentic American constitutional reality. There are several problems with interpreting these words in this manner. In the third section below, I will address the First Amendment constitutional issues directly. The first matter we will consider here, however, is that this perspective distorts and diminishes our nation's Judeo-Christian heritage that gave birth to our First Amendment privileges. If you will bear with me, I will attempt to show you why that is so.

### *The Massive Evidence of Our Nation's Judeo-Christian Heritage*
There are six specific lines of evidence I wish to share here:

### 1. *The Declaration of Independence*
Our nation was born by an explicit appeal to God. We find four instances of direct reference to deity when our founding fathers spoke their immortal words of American liberty in the Declaration of Independence:

> When in the Course of human events, it becomes necessary for one people to dissolve the political bands which have connected them with another, and to assume among the powers of the earth, the separate and equal station to which **the Laws of Nature and of Nature's God** entitle them, a decent respect to the opinions of mankind requires that they should declare the cause which impel them to the separation. We hold these truths to be self-evident, that all men are created equal, that **they are endowed by their Creator with certain unalienable Rights**, that among these are Life, Liberty and the pursuit of Happiness . . . We therefore, the Representatives of the United States of America, in General Congress, Assembled, **appealing to the Supreme Judge of the world** for the rectitude of our intentions, do, in the Name, and by Authority of the good people of these Colonies, solemnly publish and declare, That these United Colonies are, and of Right ought to be Free and Independent States; . . .And for the support of this Declaration, with a firm reliance on the **protection of divine Providence**, we mutually pledge to each other our Lives, our Fortunes and our sacred Honor.

Remember that without the Declaration of Independence, there would be no Constitution. Thus, our founding document openly and intrinsically binds law, rights, government, justice, and freedom to God. Moreover, in so doing, it explicitly incorporates several historic Judeo-Christian concepts, such as: natural law, creation, self-evident truth, equality of all men before the law, the transcendent values of "life, liberty and happiness," prayer ("appealing to the Supreme"), God's judgment of the world, and explicit trust in God's providential care in human history. Thus, in this most "public" of all American documents—for a declaration by its very nature is intended to take into account "a decent respect to the opinions of mankind"—God and the public are self-consciously intertwined. These ideas are very consistent with the two great Christian legal philosophers that especially impacted our founders—Blackstone[1] and Locke.[2]

Remember that America's Declaration of Independence tells us that the inalienable rights with which we have been endowed by our Creator include "life, liberty and the pursuit of happiness." The word "happiness" in the colonial era included reference to virtue and to the eternal salvation of one's soul in heaven.[3] Happiness was thus also the business of the church. The pursuit of happiness was the liberty to worship God according to the dictates of one's own conscience. Spiritual concerns were in the minds of our founders when they took their fateful step in July 1776. Consider that John Adams, one of our early patriots and later second president of the United States, wrote of the signing of the Declaration of Independence, that that day, "ought to be commemorated, as the Day of Deliverance, by solemn acts of devotion to God Almighty. It ought to be solemnized with pomp and parade, shows, games, sports, guns, bells, bonfires, and illuminations from one end of this continent to the other, from this time forward forevermore."*

## 2. The Signing of the Declaration of Independence

At the signing of this notable document, John Adams said:

> It is the will of Heaven that the two countries should be sundered for ever; it may be the will of Heaven that America shall suffer calamities still more wasting and distresses yet more dreadful. If this is to be the case, the furnace of affliction produces refinement in states as well as individuals; but I

submit all my hopes and fears to an overruling Providence, in which, unfashionable as the faith may be, I firmly believe.*

Samuel Adams, John's cousin and sparkplug of the Revolution said,

We have this day restored the Sovereign to Whom alone men ought to be obedient. He reigns in heaven and . . . from rising to the setting sun, may His kingdom come.[4]

*Samuel Adams – "We have this day restored the Sovereign to Whom alone men ought to be obedient. He reigns in heaven."*

John Hancock said:

Let us humbly commit our righteous cause to the great Lord of the Universe...Let us joyfully leave our concerns in the hands of Him who raises up and puts down the empires and kingdoms of the earth as He pleases.*

## 3. The Constitution of the United States of America

In fact, our Constitution does not require nor did our founders intend the removal of God from government or the public square. Our Constitution reveals explicit religious and biblical concepts. Consider the following:

the "blessings" of liberty (See Leviticus 25:10, also quoted on the
   Liberty Bell[5]);
the option to swear or affirm (See Leviticus 19:12, Numbers 30:2,
   Matthew 5:33-37, and James 5:12);
   "Sundays excepted" (See Exodus 20:8-11,

*President of the Second Continental Congress and first signer of the Declaration of Independence John Hancock – "Let us humbly commit our righteous cause to the great Lord of the Universe."*

Revelation 1:10,
    1 Corinthians 16:2, Matthew 28:1);
    "in the year of our LORD, 1787" (See Philippians 2:5-11,
    1 Corinthians 15:25-27, Revelation 19:16.)

The last argument once seemed rather petty, until one considers how many scholars today refuse to use the traditional abbreviations of B.C. and A.D., preferring instead B.C.E. (Before the Common Era) and C.E. (Common Era). It is humorous to note in our politically correct world that when one says "in the year of our LORD" (Lord is in all capital letters in the Constitution), he is simultaneously politically incorrect, but constitutional! In fact, our founders' explicit commitment to the Judeo-Christian heritage has actually been established empirically.[6] You may also wish to consider a portion of my oral testimony in the federal court case concerning the Ten Commandments on the Chester County Courthouse wall.[7]

Important expressions of the Judeo-Christian heritage surfaced in the Constitutional Convention. First was their belief in and taking account of the fallen nature of men. You undoubtedly remember the famous dictum of Lord Acton: "Power tends to corrupt and absolute power tends to corrupt absolutely." Our founders reflected this wisdom when they also consciously employed the Judeo-Christian idea of the separation of powers in their construction of the Constitution. The stakes involved in writing the Constitution were high indeed. James Madison wrote in the *National Gazette*, January 19, 1792, "Every word of [the Constitution] decides a question between power and liberty." (Padover, *The Complete Madison*, p. 335.) Because of mankind's inherent "political depravity," the three great functions of government—executive, legislative, and judicial— were punctiliously distinguished. Witness here the following from Madison's famous notes on the Constitutional Convention:

> Records of the Federal Convention, Saturday, June 30, Yates: Mr. Bedford: That all the states at present are equally sovereign and independent, has been asserted from every quarter of this house. Our deliberations here are a confirmation of the position; and I may add to it, that each of them act from interested, and many from ambitious motives. Look

at the votes which have been given on the floor of this house, and it will be found that their numbers, wealth and local views, have actuated their determination; and that the larger states proceed as if our eyes were already perfectly blinded. Impartiality, with them, is already out of the question – the reported plan is their political creed, and they support it, right or wrong ….Pretenses to support ambition are never wanting. Their cry is, where is the danger? And they insist that although the powers of the general

*Benjamin Franklin – "I therefore beg leave to move that henceforth prayers imploring the assistance of Heaven, and its blessings on our deliberations, be held in the Assembly every morning before we proceed to business."*

government will be increased, yet it will be for the good of the whole; and although the three great states form nearly a majority of the people of America, they never will hurt or injure the lesser states. I do not, gentleman trust you. If you possess the power, the abuse of it could not be checked; and what then would prevent you from exercising it to our destruction?*

The second important expression of the Judeo-Christian heritage that surfaced in the Constitutional Convention was the need for prayer. Given human self-interest and imperfection, one can also understand why Benjamin Franklin called for dependence upon divine providence and for prayer for divine assistance for the Constitutional Convention. Thus, Franklin's eloquent appeal joins together the three themes of providence, political depravity and prayer.

Mr. President,
The small progress we have made after four or five weeks close attendance & continual reasonings with each other—our different sentiments on almost

every question, several of the last producing as many noes as ays, is methinks a melancholy proof of the imperfection of the Human Understanding. We indeed seem to feel our own want of political wisdom, since we have been running about in search of it. We have gone back to ancient history for models of Government and examined the different forms of those Republics which having been formed with the seeds of their own dissolution now not longer exist. And we have viewed Modern States all round Europe, but find none of their Constitutions suitable to our circumstances.

In this situation of this Assembly, groping as it were in the dark to find political truth, and scarce able to distinguish it when presented to us, how has it happened, Sir, that we have not hitherto once thought of humbly applying to the Father of lights to illuminate our understanding? In the beginning of the Contest with G. Britain, when we were sensible of danger we had daily prayer in this room for the divine protection. –Our prayers, Sir, were heard, & they were graciously answered. All of us who were engaged in the struggle must have observed frequent instances of a superintending providence in our favor. To that kind providence we owe this happy opportunity of consulting in peace on the means of establishing our future national felicity. And have we now forgotten that powerful friend? Or do we imagine that we no longer need his assistance? I have lived, Sir, a long time, and the longer I live, the move convincing proofs I see of this truth – that God Governs in the affairs of men. And if a sparrow cannot fall to the ground without his notice, is it probable that an empire can rise without his aid? We have been assured, Sir, in the sacred writing, that "except the Lord build the House, they labour in vain that build it." I firmly believe this; and I also believe that without his concurring aid we shall succeed in this political building no better than the Builders of Babel: We shall be divided by our little partial local interests; our projects will be confounded, and we ourselves shall become a reproach and bye word down to future ages. And what is worse, mankind may hereafter from this unfortunate instance, despair of establishing Governments by Human wisdom and leave it to chance, war and conquest.

*President John Quincy Adams – "Is it not that the Declaration of Independence first organized the social compact on the foundation of the Redeemer's mission upon earth?"*

I therefore beg leave to move-that henceforth prayers imploring the assistance of Heaven, and its blessings on our deliberations, be held in the Assembly every morning before we proceed to business, and that one or more of the Clergy of this City be requested to officiate in that Service.

Mr. Sherman seconded the motion. (*The Debates in the Federal Convention of 1787 which Framed the Constitution of the United States*, Reported by James Madison, [Greenwood Press, Westport Connecticut], 181-82)

## 4. Statements of Americans and Our Christian Heritage

According to John Adams, America was born a Christian nation. He said,

The general principles, on which the Fathers achieved independence, were the only Principles in which that beautiful Assembly of young Gentlemen could Unite. . . .And what were these general

Principles? I answer, the general Principles of Christianity, in which all these Sects were United: And the general Principles of English and American Liberty, in which all those young Men United, and which had United all Parties in America, in Majorities sufficient to assert and maintain her Independence. Now I will avow, that I then believed, and now believe, that those general Principles of Christianity, are as eternal and immutable, as the Existence and Attributes of God; and that those Principles of Liberty are as unalterable as human Nature and our terrestrial, mundane system.*

Years later, John Quincy Adams, son of John Adams, and also a president of the U. S. said in an "Oration Delivered Before the Inhabitants of the Town of Newburyport":

Why is it that, next to the birthday of the Savior of the World, your most joyous and most venerated festival returns on this day [on the Fourth of July]? Is it not that, in the chain of human events, the birthday of the nation is indissolubly linked with the birthday of the Savior? That it forms a leading event in the progress of the gospel dispensation? Is it not that the Declaration of Independence first organized the social compact on the foundation of the Redeemer's mission upon earth? That it laid the cornerstone of human government upon the first precepts of Christianity?[8]

Whether we agree with Adams or not, it is telling that in 1799 the Maryland Supreme Court declared: "By our form of government, the Christian religion is the established religion; and all sects and denominations of Christians are placed on the same equal footing."* Nearly a century later in 1891, in *Church of the Holy Trinity v. The United States*, the U.S. Supreme

48

Court declared:

> Our laws and institutions must necessarily be based
> upon the teachings of the Redeemer of mankind. It
> is impossible that it should be otherwise; and in this
> sense and to this extent our civilization and our
> institutions are emphatically Christian...This is
> historically true. From the discovery of this
> continent to the present hour, there is a single
> voice making this affirmation...that this is a
> Christian nation.[9]

Consider the following summation of words from our presidents and patriots that attest to their belief in America's Christian heritage: George Washington prayed,

> . . . and finally, that he would most graciously be
> pleased to dispose us all, to do Justice, to love mercy,
> and to demean ourselves with that Charity, humility
> and pacific temper of mind, which were the
> Characteristicks of the Divine Author of our blessed
> Religion, and without an humble imitation of whose
> example in these things, we can never hope to be a
> happy Nation.*

A remarkable report was delivered on March 27, 1854, by the U.S. Congress' House Judiciary Committee:

> Had the people [the Founding Fathers], during the
> Revolution, had a suspicion of any attempt to war
> against Christianity, that Revolution would have
> been strangled in its cradle. At the time of the
> adoption of the Constitution and the amendments,
> the universal sentiment was that Christianity
> should be encouraged, but not any one sect
> [denomination]...In this age, there is no substitute

for Christianity...That was the religion of the founders of the republic, and they expected it to remain the religion of their descendants.*

Andrew Johnson said,

> Let us look forward to the time when we can take the flag of our country and nail it below the Cross, and there let it wave as it waved in the olden times, and let us gather around it and inscribe for our motto: "Liberty and Union, one and inseparable, now and forever," and exclaim, Christ first, our country next!*

Theodore Roosevelt said,

> (my) great joy and glory that, in occupying an exalted position in the nation, I am enabled, to preach the practical moralities of the Bible to my fellow-countrymen and to hold up Christ as the hope and Savior of the world. ...I believe that the next half century will determine if we will advance the cause of Christian civilization or revert to the horrors of brutal paganism.*

Woodrow Wilson said, "America was born a Christian nation. America was born to exemplify that devotion to the elements of righteousness which are derived from the revelations of Holy Scripture."*

President Harry S. Truman wrote in 1947: "This is a Christian nation."*

## 5. The Historic Idea of the "Christian Soldier" in American public life:

- General Washington gave this general order from Head Quarters in New York, on July 9, 1776, "The Colonels or commanding officers of each regiment are directed to procure Chaplains accordingly; persons of good Characters and exemplary lives—To see that all inferior officers and soldiers pay them a suitable respect and attend carefully upon religious exercises. The blessing and protection of Heaven are at all time necessary but especially so in times of public distress and danger—The General hopes and trusts, that every officer and man, will endeavour so to live, and act, as becomes a Christian Soldier defending the dearest Rights and Liberties of his country."

*President Woodrow Wilson – "America was born a Christian nation."*

- Washington's general orders on May 2, 1778, at Valley Forge declared, "While we are zealously performing the duties of good Citizens and soldiers we certainly ought not to be inattentive to the higher duties of Religion. To the distinguished Character of Patriot, it should be our highest Glory to add the more distinguished Character of Christian."

- In 1923, President Warren G. Harding said, "I rejoice particularly in the opportunity afforded me of voicing my appreciation both as President of the United Sates and as one who honestly tries to be a Christian soldier."

- In a mid-Atlantic summit, President Franklin Delano Roosevelt met with British Prime Minister Sir Winston Churchill in the darkest hours of World War II. He asked the crew of the American warship to join him in a rousing chorus of the hymn, "Onward, Christian Soldiers," after having described the United States as: "the lasting concord between men and nations, founded on the principles of Christianity." (William J. Federer, *America's God and Country*, 1994, 539)

## 6. Recent Affirmations of America's Christian Heritage

More recently, the biblical heritage of our nation was categorically affirmed by Ronald Reagan, who authorized the resolution that declared 1983 to be "The Year of the Bible." It was requested that he do so by a Joint Resolution of the 97th Congress of the United States. Resolution Public Law 97-280 declares:

WHEREAS the Bible, the Word of God, has made a unique contribution in shaping the United States as a distinctive and blessed nation and people;

WHEREAS deeply held religious convictions springing from the Holy Scriptures led to the early settlement of our Nation;

WHEREAS Biblical teachings inspired concepts of civil government that are contained in our Declaration of Independence and Constitution of the United States;

*President Ronald Reagan – 1983, The Year of the Bible*

WHEREAS many of our great national leaders – among them Presidents Washington, Jackson, Lincoln, and Wilson – paid tribute to the surpassing influence of the Bible in our country's development, as in the words of President Jackson that the Bible is "the Rock on which our Republic rests";

WHEREAS the history of our Nation clearly illustrates the value of voluntarily applying the teachings of the Scriptures in the lives of individuals, families, and societies;

WHEREAS this Nation now faces great challenges that will test the Nation as it has never been tested before; and

WHEREAS that renewing our knowledge of and faith in God through Holy Scripture can strengthen us as a nation and a people:

NOW, THEREFORE, be it

Resolved by the Senate and House of Representatives of the United States of America in Congress assembled, That the president is authorized and requested to designate 1983 as a national "Year of the Bible" in recognition of both the formative influence the Bible has been for our Nation, and our national need to study and apply the teachings of the Holy Scriptures.

Thomas P. O'Neill
Speaker of the House

Strom Thurmond
President of the
Senate – Pro Tempore

Approved October 4, 1982
Ronald Reagan

No wonder French, political scientist Alexis De Tocqueville wrote, "Christianity, therefore, reigns without any obstacle, by universal consent; the consequence is, as I have before observed, that every principle of the moral world is fixed and determinate."*

As we conclude the discussion of your first question, I hope you will at least be prepared to acknowledge that our founders and the subsequent Judeo-Christian heritage of American history sow no seeds of conflict with the concept that our nation is "under God." They saw no inherent contradiction of affirming the First Amendment and its religious liberties and calling on Americans to acknowledge that these liberties come from God.

With these initial remarks reflecting on our founders' understanding of the legitimate role of God in the public forum of government, let us consider another of your important concerns.

# chapter 3

# THE TEN
# COMMANDMENTS
# AND THE COURTHOUSE

Can religious documents be used in
governmental settings for secular purpose?

"Likewise, I have trouble understanding why there was an
uproar over the decision to remove the Ten Commandments
plaque from the Chester County Courthouse."[10]

## THE COMMANDMENTS

THOU SHALT HAVE NO OTHER GODS BEFORE ME.

THOU SHALT NOT MAKE UNTO THEE ANY GRAVEN IMAGE, OR ANY LIKENESS OF ANY THING THAT IS IN HEAVEN ABOVE, OR THAT IS IN THE EARTH BENEATH, OR THAT IS IN THE WATER UNDER THE EARTH:

THOU SHALT NOT BOW DOWN THYSELF TO THEM, NOR SERVE THEM: For I the Lord thy God am a jealous God, visiting the iniquity of the fathers upon the children unto the third and fourth generation of them that hate me, and shewing mercy unto thousands of them that love me, and keep my commandments.

THOU SHALT NOT TAKE THE NAME OF THE LORD THY GOD IN VAIN; For the Lord will not hold him guiltless that taketh His name in vain.

REMEMBER THE SABBATH DAY, TO KEEP IT HOLY.

SIX DAYS SHALT THOU LABOR AND DO ALL THY WORK:

BUT THE SEVENTH DAY IS THE SABBATH OF THE LORD THY GOD: IN IT THOU SHALT NOT DO ANY WORK, THOU, NOR THY SON, NOR THY DAUGHTER, THY MANSERVANT, NOR THY MAIDSERVANT, NOR THY CATTLE, NOR THY STRANGER THAT IS WITHIN THY GATES: For in six days the Lord made heaven and earth, the sea, and all that in them is, and rested the seventh day, wherefore the Lord blessed the sabbath day, and hallowed it.

HONOR THY FATHER AND THY MOTHER; That thy days may be long upon the land which the Lord thy God giveth thee

THOU SHALT NOT KILL.

THOU SHALT NOT COMMIT ADULTERY.

THOU SHALT NOT STEAL.

THOU SHALT NOT BEAR FALSE WITNESS AGAINST THY NEIGHBOUR.

THOU SHALT NOT COVET THY NEIGHBOUR'S HOUSE.

THOU SHALT NOT COVET THY NEIGHBOUR'S WIFE, NOR HIS MAN — SERVANT, NOR HIS MAIDSERVANT, NOR HIS OX, NOR HIS ASS, NOR ANY THING THAT IS THY NEIGHBOUR'S.

### SUMMARY

THOU SHALT LOVE THE LORD THY GOD WITH ALL THINE HEART, AND WITH ALL THY SOUL AND WITH ALL THY MIND.

THOU SHALT LOVE THY NEIGHBOUR AS THYSELF.

*The Ten Commandments plaque at the Chester County Courthouse in Pennsylvania*

Your comment raises the question of the legitimacy of displaying the Ten Commandments in public settings or, can "religious" documents be used in governmental settings or on government property for secular purposes.

I respond to your difficulty in understanding the "uproar" over the decision to remove the Ten Commandments plaque from the Chester County Courthouse, by asking you to consider with me three important issues: (1) Our nation's historical precedents; (2) The problem of judicial activism vis-à-vis free speech or what we might call religious/cultural censorship; and (3) The need for transcendent law in our age of moral confusion.

### (1) Our nation's historical precedents with respect to religion and morality in the public arena.

Pennsylvania is the land set aside by William Penn for his "Holy Experiment" in religious liberty.[11] It is significant that the first legislative act of Pennsylvania passed at Chester on December 7, 1682, included a bold statement of the importance of God in human government: "Whereas the glory of Almighty God and the good of mankind, is the reason and end of government, and therefore, government in itself is a venerable Ordinance of God."

Retiring President George Washington in his Farewell Address to the American nation acknowledged the essential unity of Americans in regard to religion at our nation's beginning. He declared,

> For this you have every inducement of sympathy and interest. Citizens, by birth or choice, of a common country that country has a right to concentrate your affections. The name of American, which belongs to you in your national capacity, must always exalt the just pride of patriotism more than any appellation derived from local discriminations. **With slight shades of difference, you have the same religion, manners, habits, and political principles.** You have in a common cause fought and triumphed together; the independence and liberty you possess are the work of joint councils, and joint efforts of common dangers, sufferings,

and successes. (Emphasis added)

But while affirming such unity in the political-ethical arena of America, Washington was not implying that all held to the same religious tenets. Rejecting any form of anti-religious sentiment, his timeless words to the Jewish Congregation in Newport, Rhode Island, dated August 17, 1790, still ring true to the American ideal:

> The Citizens of the United States of America have a right to applaud themselves for having given to Mankind examples of an enlarged and liberal policy, a policy worthy of imitation. All possess alike liberty of conscience and immunities of citizenship. It is now no more that toleration is spoken of, as if it was by the indulgence of one class of people, that another enjoyed the exercise of their inherent natural rights. For happily the Government of the United States, which gives to bigotry no sanction, to persecution no assistance, requires only that they who live under its protection should demean themselves as good citizens, in giving it on all occasions their effectual support.[12]

Washington thus simultaneously recognized America's religious heritage as essentially Judeo-Christian and America's commitment to respect religious diversity. In fact, President Washington said that what makes for good citizens is "religion and morality." Consider his Farewell Address:

> Of all the dispositions and habits which lead to political prosperity, **religion and morality are indispensable supports**. In vain would that man claim the tribute of patriotism, who should labor to subvert **these great pillars of human happiness,—** these firmest props of the duties of men and citizens. The mere politician, equally with the pious man, ought to respect and to cherish them. A volume

could not trace all their connections with private and public felicity. Let it simply be asked, Where is the security for property, for reputation, for life, if the sense of religious obligation desert the oaths which are the instruments of investigation in courts of justice? **And let us with caution indulge the supposition that morality can be maintained without religion**. Whatever may be conceded to the influence of refined education on minds of peculiar structure, **reason and experience both forbid us to expect that national morality can prevail in exclusion of religious principle**.

'Tis substantially true, that **virtue or morality is a necessary spring of popular government**. The rule, indeed, extends with more or less force to every species of free government. (Emphasis added)

Clearly Washington believed freedom of conscience and the emphasis on religion and morality to be compatible and necessary concerns in the American government. Under the rule of the Constitution and the First Amendment, even in the context of divergent faith traditions, President Washington saw the need for the virtue and morality supported by religion if there was to be stability in constitutional government. It is this very balance that Washington desired that the plaque on the courthouse wall in West Chester maintains.

This answers the complaint of the detractors of the Ten Commandments plaque that claims The Decalogue is a profoundly religious text and thus cannot be in a public place. Admittedly, the commandments are religious. But the question here is whether the religious character of the commandments is such that they violate the intent of the First Amendment, if they are employed or displayed by civil government. Our answer here is perhaps best given by those who were the founders of our American republic and had a direct hand in writing, defending, adopting, and implementing the Constitution and the First Amendment.

Gouverneur Morris (1752-1816), writer of the final draft of the Constitution of the United States, being the head of the Committee on Style, was the originator of the phrase "We the people of the United States." He was

*Gouverneur Morris – "Education should teach the precepts of religion, and the duties of man toward God."*

thirty-five years old when he served as one of the members of the Continental Congress. He spoke 173 times during the constitutional debates (more than any other delegate). He declared, "Religion is the only solid basis of good morals; therefore, education should teach the precepts of religion, and the duties of man toward God."*

In his First Inaugural Address, Washington stated:

. . . it would be peculiarly improper to omit, in this first official act, my fervent supplications to that Almighty Being, who rules over the universe, who presides in the councils of nations.... No people can be bound to acknowledge and adore the Invisible Hand which conducts the affairs of men more than the people of the United States. Every step by which they have advanced to the character of an independent nation seems to have been distinguished by some token of providential agency. . . . We ought to be no less persuaded that the propitious smiles of Heaven can never be expected on a nation that disregards the eternal rules of order and right which Heaven itself has ordained.

Benjamin Rush (1745-1813) was a physician, signer of the Declaration of Independence, Surgeon General of the Continental Army, a writer of the Pennsylvania Constitution and later helped found the first American anti-slavery society. In 1798, after the adoption of the Constitution, Rush declared: "The only foundation for...a republic is to be laid in Religion. Without this there can be no virtue, and without virtue there can be no liberty, and liberty is the object and life of all republican governments."*

Our second president, John Adams declared in his address to the military dated October 11, 1798:

> We have no government armed with power capable
> of contending with human passions unbridled by
> morality and religion. Avarice, ambition, revenge, or
> gallantry, would break the strongest cords of our
> Constitution as a whale goes through a net. Our
> Constitution was made only for a moral and
> religious people. It is wholly inadequate to the
> government of any other. [13]

Similarly on August 28, 1811, Adams wrote:

> Religion and virtue are the only foundations, not
> only of republicanism and of all free government,
> but of social felicity under all governments and in
> all the combinations of human society.*

The Northwest Ordinance was adopted by the United States Congress in
1787. It enabled the eventual creation of our states northwest of the Ohio
River. Its provisions were intended to be binding upon America. Those
provisions also declare a perpetual and legitimate
state interest in religion.

> It is hereby ordained and
> declared by the authority
> aforesaid, That the
> following articles shall be
> considered as articles of
> compact between the
> original States and the
> people and States in the said
> territory and forever remain
> unalterable, unless by common
> consent, to wit: . . .
>     Art. 3rd. Religion,

*Benjamin Rush –"The only foundation
for . . . a republic is to be laid in Religion."*

morality and knowledge, being necessary to good government and the happiness of mankind, schools and the means of education shall forever be encouraged.[14]

*President James Madison – "The belief in a God All Powerful wise and good, is so essential to the moral order of the World.*

Nearly thirty years after the adoption of the Northwest Ordinance, James Madison, the author of the First Amendment, and great defender of the liberty of the conscience said on November 20, 1825:

The belief in a God All Powerful wise and good, is so essential to the moral order of the World and to the happiness of man, that arguments which enforce it cannot be drawn from too many sources nor adapted with too much solicitude to the different characters and capacities to be impressed with it.[15]

But this understanding of the law did not disappear with the age of our founders. President Franklin D. Roosevelt explained:

The skeptics and the cynics of Washington's day did not believe that ordinary men and women have the capacity for freedom and self-government. They said that liberty and equality were idle dreams that could not come true—just as today there are many Americans who sneer at the determination to attain freedom from want and freedom from fear, on the ground that these are ideals which can never be realized. They say it is ordained that we must always have poverty, and that we must always have war. You know; they are like the people who carp at the Ten Commandments because some people are in the habit of breaking one or more of them.*

President Harry S. Truman affirmed:

> The fundamental basis of this nation's laws was given to Moses on the Mount. The fundamental basis of our Bill of Rights comes from the teachings we get from Exodus and St. Matthew, from Isaiah and St. Paul. I don't think we emphasize that enough these days. If we don't have a proper fundamental moral background, we will finally end up with a totalitarian government which does not believe in rights for anybody except the State!*

Similarly, in his Inaugural Address, January 20, 1961, President John F. Kennedy proclaimed: "The rights of man come not from the generosity of the state but from the hand of God."

The civil religion of liberty and morality described by our American leaders from the past could well be summarized in the commandments on the wall of the courthouse in West Chester, Pennsylvania. Perhaps it would be wise for Chester County to let this expression of our nation's founding values remain in the public eye.

All this corroborates Supreme Court Justice Douglas' remark, "We are a religious people whose institutions presuppose a Supreme Being."* Our founders believed that the civil religion that enabled the American republic to exist was a religion marked by morality, and this morality was contained in the Ten Commandments.

*President Harry S. Truman – "The fundamental basis of our Bill of Rights comes from the teachings we get from Exodus and St. Matthew, from Isaiah and St. Paul."*

## (2) Judicial activism is weakening our free speech by religious and cultural censorship.

I fully affirm that Americans must protect

the right to nontheistic belief and speech, but that is not the fundamental problem here. Free speech is guaranteed to all. No one is required to profess the Ten Commandments as their faith, nor to say the pledge to "one nation under God." But what is at stake is whether people of faith have lost their right to do so if they, as citizens, desire to do so, consistent with the historical heritage of our nation's founders and founding documents.

My concern is simply this: No one, whether theist or non-theist, acting through the courts, may change the constitutional perspective of American government, whether in the enabling document of the United States, The Declaration of Independence, or the Constitution itself. President George Washington emphasized this when he said in his Farewell Address at the end of his second term as president,

> The basis of our political systems is the right of the people to make and to alter their constitutions of government. But the Constitution which at any time exists till changed by an explicit and authentic act of the whole people is sacredly obligatory upon all. The very idea of the power and the right of the people to establish government presupposed the duty of every individual to obey the established government.

The balance required of us here, then, is a protection of non-theistic faith, simultaneously with recognition of the truth of Justice Douglas' remark. For a federal judge to make a ruling to remove the plaque, without considering the will of the people of the community and by disregarding the intent and express declarations of the founders and authors of our constitutional documents, is a form of judicial tyranny inconsistent with the spirit and laws of our free people and our nation's heritage. "We are a religious people whose institutions presuppose a Supreme Being." Leaving the plaque on the wall does exactly that.

### (3) The need for transcendent law in our age of moral confusion.

But what was true for our founders' is true for us today. We still need morality and religion for the support of our government and Constitution, if we hope to remain a free people. Upon leaving one of the many sessions of the Constitutional Convention held in Philadelphia in 1787, Benjamin Franklin, one of the delegates, was asked what type of government was being considered for America. "A Republic, if you can keep it" was his reply.

In the place of our nation's recognition of the importance of a transcendent law, recognition of transcendent values, "inalienable rights," will help us "keep it." However, there has been placed upon our public life the narrow interests of a secular humanist perspective that demands everyone in public discourse to shed their God-given

*US Supreme Court Justice William O. Douglas – "We are a religious people whose institutions presuppose a Supreme Being."*

liberties of free speech and the free exercise of religion when they enter the public square. This perspective mandates that all conform to the atheist creed that teaches that God is non-existent and certainly not relevant. Thus, John Adams' statement made on June 20, 1815 is still pertinent: "The question before the human race is, whether the God of nature shall govern the world by His own laws..."

Similarly, in his Inaugural Address, January 20, 1961, President John F. Kennedy proclaimed: "The rights of man come not from the generosity of the state, but from the hand of God."

Without a sound moral structure, we will continue to face the erosion of the moral order of our culture. In the wake of the Columbine shootings, the Oklahoma City bombing, the explosive tragedies of 9/11 in New York City, at the Pentagon, and in the open field of the crash site in rural Pennsylvania, should we not recognize that the principles of "Thou shalt not kill" and "Thou shalt love they neighbor as thyself" have never made more common sense for the public square than today?

Patrick Henry correctly warned future Americans,

> Bad men cannot make good citizens. It is impossible that a nation of infidels or idolaters should be a nation of free men. It is when a people forget God

that tyrants forge their chains. A vitiated state of morals, a corrupted public conscience, are incompatible with freedom. No free government or the blessings of liberty can be preserved to any people but by a firm adherence to justice, moderation, temperance, frugality, and virtue, and by a frequent recurrence to fundamental Principles.[16]

Our second president, John Adams wrote on August 28, 1811:

Religion and virtue are the only foundations, not only of republicanism and of all free government, but of social felicity under all governments and in all the combinations of human society."

In Adams' correspondence to Thomas Jefferson we find:

Have you ever found in history, one single example of a Nation thoroughly corrupted that was afterwards restored to virtue?...And without virtue, there can be no political liberty...Will you tell me how to prevent riches from becoming the effects of temperance and industry? Will you tell me how to prevent luxury from producing effeminacy, intoxication, extravagance, vice and folly? ...I believe no effort in favour of virtue is lost. . . .

The Ten Commandments and the Sermon on the Mount contain my religion. . . November 4, 1816.*

President Theodore Roosevelt clearly understood the impact of the High Court's removal of the Ten Commandments would have on public life. In 1910 he said,

Every thinking man, when he thinks, realizes that the teachings of the Bible are so interwoven and entwined with our whole civic and social life that it would be literally impossible for us to figure ourselves what that life would be if these standards were removed. We would lose almost all the standards by which we now judge both public and private morals; all the standards towards which we, with more or less resolution, strive to raise ourselves.*

You have affirmed your trouble in understanding why there was an uproar over the decision to remove the Ten Commandments plaque from the Chester Country Courthouse. My understanding of our nation's founders and their explicit declaration of their Judeo-Christian heritage is that they would have been troubled if there had been *no* uproar by those who wish to maintain their careful balance of "inalienable rights" and freedom flowing from their recognition of one God.

But more, they also anticipated the inevitable "uproars" of a society that abandoned the moral supports of their carefully crafted constitutional government. My prayer is that our departure from fundamental public and private morality will not accelerate the inevitable cultural explosions worldwide, illustrated by Oklahoma City, Columbine, the World Trade Center, and the tragic murders of Amish school children in idyllic Lancaster County, Pennsylvania. Ultimately, we pursue these foundational values of the Judeo-Christian faith not just for ourselves, but for the stability of the whole world.

# chapter 4

# THE
# SEPARATION OF
# CHURCH AND STATE:

The relationship of church and state
in the American context.

"I see two problems with this blending of church and state."

Your comment raises the question of what is the proper relationship of church and state in the American context. As we pursue this question, I will raise these issues, (1) our high court's historical understanding of the First Amendment, (2) how we got our Constitution (3) how we got the Bill of Rights with its First Amendment (4) the metaphorical Jeffersonian wall of separation between church and state (5) the "blending" of church and state vs. the cooperation of church and state (6) the enabling of religious pluralism based on the values of the Ten Commandments.

## (1) Our High Court's Historical Understanding of the First Amendment.

Scholars have discussed the melding of religious liberty with an appropriate recognition of God in the public square of government that I have been describing here. It has been termed America's commitment to a "benevolent pluralism" and a "common sense" approach to the First Amendment. I believe this view has characterized American liberty from its inception up until the mid-twentieth century. This is especially well reflected by Justice Douglas. Speaking for a majority of his brethren, in 1952 he discussed what he termed the "common sense" of the American principle of separation. In essence it is this: "The First Amendment does not say that in every and all respects there shall be a separation of Church and State."*

Mark Howe explains:

> He [Justice Douglas] went on to acknowledge that if absolutes rather than common sense were to shape our constitutional law, prayers in our legislative halls; the appeals to the Almighty in the messages of the Chief Executive; the proclamations making Thanksgiving Day a holiday; "so help me God" in our courtroom oaths – these and all other references to the Almighty that run through our laws, our public rituals, our ceremonies would be flouting the First Amendment. A fastidious atheist or agnostic could even object to the supplication with which the Court opens each session: "God save the United States and this Honorable Court." The Justice

recognized, however, that any reading of the First Amendment which would compel the condemnation of the traditional religious ways of the American people and its governments should be avoided. He crowned his exemplifications of the... tolerance resulting from the exercise of common sense with the homely piety: "We are a religious people whose institutions presuppose a Supreme Being." (Mark Howe, in *The Garden of the Wilderness* (Chicago: University of Chicago Press, 1965)

Simply put, the interpretation of the First Amendment that underlies your concern is recent, and as a departure from our founders' legacy is novel and essentially unhistorical. Supreme Court Justice William Rehnquist in his dissenting opinion in *Wallace v. Jaffree* on June 1985 put it very succinctly:

The "wall of separation between church and state" is a metaphor based on bad history, a metaphor which has proved useless as a guide to judging. It should be frankly and explicitly abandoned.

*US Supreme Court Chief Justice William H. Rehnquist – "The 'wall of separation between church and state' is a metaphor based on bad history."*

Consider also the 1984 Supreme Court decision of *Lynch v. Donnelly*:

The Constitution [does not] require complete separation of church and state; it affirmatively mandates accommodation, not mere tolerance, of all religions, and forbids hostility toward any.... Anything less would require the callous indifference we have said was never intended by the Establishment Clause. Indeed, we have observed such hostility would bring us into war with our national tradition as embodied in the First Amendment's guarantee of the free exercise of religion.

## (2) How We Got Our Constitution

The Articles of Confederation were finally adopted in 1781. This first form of American government enabled the new nation to wage the war to secure its independence. However, the articles showed obvious areas of weakness, which threatened the unity and strength of the new nation, eventually leading to the calling of the Constitutional Convention.

In May 1787, forty-two delegates arrived in Philadelphia to try to craft a constitution for the thirteen states. Much debate ensued, with leading figures of the Revolution participating, including George Washington, Benjamin Franklin, as well as new, younger thinkers James Madison and Alexander Hamilton. Indeed, the eighty-one year old Franklin was the American patriarch at the time of the Constitutional Convention held at Independence Hall in Philadelphia in 1787. In a most remarkable way, he hallowed the Convention with his eloquent call for prayer. Addressing the Convention, presided over by none other than George Washington, he reminded those in attendance of God's sovereign providence on America's behalf:

> In the beginning of the Contest with Great Britain, when we were sensible of danger we had daily prayer in this room for the Divine protection —— Our prayers, Sir, were heard, and they were graciously answered. All of us who were engaged in the struggle must have observed frequent instances of a superintending providence in our favor.
>
> To that kind providence we owe this happy opportunity of consulting in peace on means of establishing our future national felicity. And have we now forgotten that powerful Friend? Or do we imagine we no longer need His assistance?
>
> I have lived, Sir, a long time, and the longer I live, the more convincing proofs I see of this truth: that God governs in the affairs of man. And if a

> sparrow cannot fall to the ground without his notice
> is it probable that an empire can rise without His
> aid? We have been assured sir, in the Sacred
> Writings that "except the Lord build the house, they
> labour in vain that build it" (Psalm 127:1). I firmly
> believe this, and I also believe that without His
> concurring aid we shall succeed in this political
> building no better than the builder of Babel. We
> shall be divided by our little partial local interests;
> our projects will be confounded and we ourselves
> shall become a reproach and bye word down to
> future ages. I therefore beg leave to move that,
> henceforth, prayers imploring the assistance of
> Heaven and its blessing on our deliberation be held
> in this assembly every morning. . and that one or
> more of the clergy of this city be requested to
> officiate in that service.*

General Washington was selected to preside over the Constitutional Convention. He set the tone of the gathering soon after his arrival in Philadelphia. "If to please the people we offer what we ourselves disapprove, how can we afterwards defend our work? Let us raise a standard to which the wise and the honest can repair; the event is in the hands of God."* The stakes were high indeed. James Madison wrote in the *National Gazette*, January 19, 1792, "Every word of [the Constitution] decides a question between power and liberty."*

Looking back at the Constitutional Convention, from the vantage point of the following summer, Washington saw God's intervention in the production of the American Constitution. On June 30, 1788, after the ratification of the Constitution, Washington wrote to Benjamin Lincoln:

> No Country upon Earth ever had it more in its
> power to attain these blessings ... Much to be
> regretted indeed would it be, were we to neglect the
> means and depart from the road which Providence
> has pointed us to, so plainly; I cannot believe it will

ever come to pass. The Great Governor of the
Universe has led us too long and too far ... to
forsake us in the midst of it. . . We may, now and
then, get bewildered; but I hope and trust that there
is good sense and virtue enough left to recover the
right path.

In fact, Washington wrote to his dear French friend and fellow warrior
Marquis de LaFayette calling the Constitution a "miracle."* Similarly, General
Washington noted "Should everything proceed as we anticipate, it will be so
much beyond anything we had a right to imagine or expect eighteen months
ago that it will demonstrate the finger of Providence in human affairs greater
than any event in history." James Madison also considered the Constitution to
be the result of a miracle. In a letter to Jefferson he says, "It is impossible to
consider the degree of concord which ultimately prevailed as less than a
miracle."* During the convention, Alexander Hamilton was summarized by
Madison:

This was the critical moment for forming such a
Government. We should run every risk in trusting
to future amendments. As yet we retain the habits of
union. We are weak & sensible of our weakness.

*What do we mean when we say that first of all we seek liberty? I often
wonder whether we do not rest our hopes too much upon constitutions,
upon laws, and upon courts. These are false hopes; believe me, these are
false hopes. Liberty lies in the hearts of men and women; when it dies
there, no constitution, no law, no court can save it; no constitution, no
law, no court can even do much to help it. While it lies there, it needs no
constitution, no law, no court to save it.*

*Justice Learned Hand*
*The Spirit of Liberty Speech*
*1944, I Am an American Day*

Henceforward the motives will become feebler, and the difficulties greater. It is a miracle that we are now here exercising our tranquil & free deliberations on the subject. It would be madness to trust to future miracles. A thousand causes must obstruct a reproduction of them.*

Not every delegate was satisfied, but on March 4, 1789, the day which had been chosen to be the starting point of a new federal government, eleven states had ratified the Constitution. North Carolina and Rhode Island ratified it in November 1789 and May 1790, respectively. The Preamble of the Constitution highlights the quest for and value of the "Blessings of Liberty":

We the People of the United States, in Order to form a more perfect Union, establish Justice, insure domestic Tranquility, provide for the common defence, promote the general Welfare, and secure the Blessings of Liberty to ourselves and our Posterity, do ordain and establish this Constitution for the United States of America.

### (3) How We Got The Bill of Rights With Its First Amendment

Of much debate surrounding the new Constitution, however, was the lack of a Bill of Rights. Having not yet forgotten the search for religious and civil freedom that had been the impetus for the pilgrim journey in the first place, there were those who felt strongly that a Bill of Rights was essential to protect the citizens from the return of a tyrannical government.

James Wilson and John Smilie debated the need for such a document in November 1787. James Wilson, as a signer of the Constitution, asserted that it was unnecessary, because any power not expressly given to the government in the Constitution would be understood to be reserved for the people. John Smilie vehemently disagreed, noting that,

So loosely, so inaccurately are the powers which are enumerated in this constitution defined, that it will be impossible, without a test of that kind, to

> *"The United States furnished the first example in history of a government deliberately depriving itself of all legislative control over religion."\**
>
> *Philip Schaff,*
> *Church Historian*

ascertain the limits of authority, and to declare when government has degenerated into oppression…. At present there is no security, even for the rights of conscience, and under the sweeping force of the sixth article, every principle of a bill of rights, every stipulation of the most sacred and invaluable privileges of man, are left to the mercy of government.*

Further impetus for the crafting of a Bill of Rights was the existence of such a document in Virginia. James Madison's ideas of religious liberty had developed under Thomas Jefferson's significant influence.[17] Jefferson's text for *An Act for Establishing Religious Liberty*, written some years earlier, was successfully brought to adoption under Madison's leadership in the Virginia Legislature in 1786. This was only a year before the adoption of the U. S. Constitution, and five years before the adoption of our First Amendment in 1791. Jefferson's *Act* declares:

> Whereas Almighty God hath created the mind free; that all attempts to influence it by temporal punishments or burthens, or by civil incapacitations, tend only to beget habits of hypocrisy and meaness, and are a departure from the plan of the Holy author of our religion, who being Lord both of body and mind, yet chose not to propagate it by coercions on either, as was in his Almighty power to do; that the impious presumption of legislators and rulers, civil as well as ecclesiastical, who being themselves but fallible and uninspired men, have assumed dominion over the faith of others, setting up their

own opinions and modes of thinking as the only true and infallible, and as such endeavouring to impose them on others, hath established and maintained false religions over the greatest part of the world, and through all time; ....Be it enacted by the General Assembly, That no man shall be compelled to frequent or support any religious worship, place or ministry whatsoever, nor shall be enforced, restrained, molested, or burthened in his body or goods, nor shall otherwise suffer on account of his religious opinions or belief; but that all men shall be free to profess, and by argument to maintain, their opinion in matters of religion, and that the same shall in no wise diminish, enlarge, or affect their civil capacities.[18]

James Madison, with the aid of several others, also developed the language of the First Amendment. In a letter sent to James Madison on February 28, 1788 entitled "John Leland's Objections to the Constitution without a Bill of Rights," Reverend Leland states:

What is clearest of all, Religious Liberty is not sufficiently secured; No Religious test is Required as a qualification to fill any office under the United States, but if a Majority of Congress with the President favour one System more then another, they may oblige all others to pay to the support of their System as much as they please, and if oppression does not ensue, it will be owing to the Mildness of Administration and not to any Constitutional defence, and if the Manners of People are so far Corrupted, that they cannot live by Republican principles, it is Very Dangerous leaving Religious Liberty at their mercy.[19]

A careful reading of the First Amendment shows us that the concern that motivated our founders was not to keep church and state separate, but to protect the conscience from governmental encroachments. Twenty iterations of the language for the First Amendment ensued in the congressional debate before the final version that we now know as the First Amendment was sent to the House on September 24, 1789: **"Congress shall make no Law respecting an establishment of Religion, or prohibiting the free exercise thereof." (emphasis added)**[20] It is worthy of note, that not once in any of those twenty attempts to write the language of the First Amendment did the phrase "separation of Church and State" appear! The word "conscience," although it does not appear in the final form, occurs in twelve of these proposed iterations. Thus, it is evident that the motivating concern of the drafters of the First Amendment was to protect conscience from government, not to protect government from religion. Within two years, ten amendments, known as the Bill of Rights, was approved, providing the foundation for the protection of the fundamental rights and liberties we now enjoy in America.

### (4) The Metaphorical Jeffersonian Wall of Separation between Church and State

In fact, the source for this idea of the separation of church and state is not the Constitution, but a private letter of Thomas Jefferson. Sadly, the use of this letter is also historically incorrect. The focus of Jefferson's letter was also protecting the conscience. This focus of protecting the conscience is also seen when Jefferson's famous language of the "wall of separation between Church and State" is quoted in context. In his letter to a committee of the Danbury Baptist Association, Connecticut, January 1, 1802, Jefferson declared:

> Believing with you that religion is a matter which lies solely between man and his God, that he owes account to none other for his faith or his worship, that the legislative powers of government reach actions only, and not opinions, I contemplate with sovereign reverence that act of the whole American people which declared that their legislature should "make no law respecting an establishment of religion, or prohibiting the free exercise thereof," thus building a wall of separation between Church

and State. Adhering to the expression of the supreme will of the nation in behalf of the rights of conscience, I shall see with sincere satisfaction the progress of those sentiments which tend to restore to man all his natural rights, convinced he has not natural right in opposition to his social duties.[21]

Religious liberty in its basic form was completed in America after various historic denominations rewrote their creeds and forms of governments so that they would reflect the American federal constitutional system of the non-establishment, yet free exercise of religion.[22] All the state churches, including those of New England, were ultimately disestablished to conform to the freedom of religion on the federal level. Many state constitutions explicitly include the language to protect the rights of Conscience.[23]

It is ironic that the language of "separation between church and state," although not appearing in the First Amendment of our U.S. Constitution, was included in the Constitution of the former U. S. S. R.:

In order to ensure to citizens freedom of conscience, the church in the U.S.S.R. is separated from the State, and the school from the church. Freedom of religious worship and freedom of anti-religious propaganda is recognized for all citizens."[24]

The result of misreading the Jeffersonian metaphor of "separation of Church and State" into our First Amendment has

*...the care of souls is not committed to the civil magistrate, any more than to other men. It is not committed unto him, I say, but God; because it appears not that God has ever given any such authority to one man over another, as to compel any one to his religion.*

*John Locke*
*A Letter Concerning Toleration**

been the granting of expansive powers to our courts. Accordingly, our courts have lost the historic First Amendment's focus on conscience. The immediate result? The courts (like the Ninth Circuit) declare that it is unconstitutional to teach in a public setting (even if it is in the Declaration) that a nation only has certain unalienable rights, if it has been so endowed by God the Creator. Similarly, some are forbidden to say God's name when they pledge their allegiance to our nation, even if their consciences permit them to agree with this act established by our own Congress in accord with our national heritage.

To forbid speaking of God certainly protects the consciences of atheists. Does it protect the free speech and the consciences of theists? The historic pattern protected the rights of atheists as well, for their free speech has also been honored. The historic American understanding of First Amendment liberties was well explained in 1876 by theologian Charles Hodge:

> In the process of time thousands have come among us, who are neither Protestants nor Christians...All are welcomed; all are admitted to equal rights and privileges. All are allowed to worship as they please, or not to worship at all, if they see fit. No man is molested for his religion or for his want of religion. No man is required to profess any form of faith, or to join any religious association. More than this cannot reasonably be demanded. More, however, is demanded. The infidel demands that the government should be conducted on the principle that Christianity is false. The atheist demands that it should be conducted on the assumption that there is no God, and the positivist on the principle that men are not free agents. The sufficient answer to all this is that it cannot possibly be done.*

## (5) The "Blending" of Church and State vs. the Cooperation of Church and State

There are indeed real tensions between nontheistic faiths and America's theistic and Judeo-Christian beliefs enshrined in our founding documents: The Declaration of Independence,[25] and in our national motto, our national anthem,[26] our national seal,[27] and our pledge to the flag.[28]

But the real question, as I see it, is not whether our public school children should be permitted and encouraged to say the Pledge of Allegiance, but do our courts have the authority to forbid Americans in any public setting from saying the pledge? Do our courts have a constitutional right to require Americans in government or in public to act in a manner contrary to what Justice Douglas asserted in 1952, namely that "We are a religious people whose institutions presuppose a Supreme Being."*

There is confusion here between what you call the "blending of church and state" and what I would call "the *cooperation* of church and state." This difference is an important one, and it largely flows from one's understanding of "the separation of church and state." Actually the separation of church and state can either be a friendly or a hostile separation. Accordingly, Philip Wogman offers four basic types of church-state relationships:

1.  Theocracy: The state is under the control of religious leaders or institutions for religious purposes.
2.  Erastianism: The church under the control of the state has been termed "Erastianism" (after the sixteenth-century, Swiss-German, Thomas Erastes).
3.  Separation of church and state—friendly: Religious and political institutions are legally separate but not hostile to each other.
4.  Separation of Church and state—unfriendly: Religious and political institutions are legally separate and in an antagonistic relationship.[29]

What I think often happens is that those who hold to an "unfriendly" separation of church and state hear the phrases "cooperation of church and state," or a "friendly" separation of church and state, but they immediately think "theocracy." Just so you have no doubt about my intent, I am in support of the separation of church and state; that is, I am opposed to both theocracy and Erastianism. But I see church and state as friendly neighbors living on the opposite side of a chest-high "wall of separation," to use Jefferson's metaphor. Both need to cooperate, or neither will do their jobs as well as they ought.

This is especially so today, given all that is wrong with our "sweet land of liberty": drugs; kids shooting kids, their parents and their teachers; teen suicides; schools out of control; the disintegration of the family, just to name but a few. Freedom seems to ring less and less while police sirens seem to wail more and more.

I do not desire a blending of church and state. What would a blending of church and state look like? Take a look at any nation with an established church and you will see what it would mean: taxes paid by nonadherents of the state religion to support the state religion, and sometimes the use of the coercive power of government to force compliance. We see this reality in the Muslim states where the Qur'an is enforced by the power of government.

But if we might have to fear "blending of church and state," which to me seems very far away on the horizon of real possibilities in the U.S.A., we do have to fear the "unfriendly" separation of church and state: Simply consider the realities of religious persecution worldwide and the rising specter of government "sect lists" in western European countries like France and eastern European countries as well.

Depictions of the Ten Commandments in the US Supreme Court building

### (6) The Enabling of Religious Pluralism Based on the Values of the Ten Commandments

As Americans of all faiths who have said or in conscience who have chosen not to say the Pledge, our nation has advanced religious liberty worldwide and at home for all. Why do we fear the very solution that has brought healing to religious bigotry in America and is seeking to do so worldwide? Through the decades that the plaque of the Ten Commandments has been on the courthouse wall, America has provided more religious liberty at home and encouragement for it abroad than any other nation on earth. I believe the principle of loving one's neighbor imbedded in the Ten Commandments is one of the reasons why this is so.

The point I wish to emphasize is that it is the Judeo-Christian heritage of religious liberty and justice reflected by the courthouse's cultural/historical use of the commandments that has made this pluralism with freedom possible. Given the positive good promoted by our founders' use of the commandments, and the religious liberty and pluralism they have fostered, are we sure that taking them down will improve our most fortunate American experience? The common sense approach is to assert our religious pluralism, and also to permit the historical and traditional words of the commands to stand. William Penn named his city Philadelphia, since it was to be marked by religious liberty. Philadelphia, of course, means the City of Brotherly Love. The summary of the commandments on the courthouse wall declares: THOU SHALT LOVE THE LORD THY GOD WITH ALL THINE HEART, AND WITH ALL THY SOUL AND WITH ALL THY MIND. THOU SHALT LOVE THY NEIGHBOUR AS THYSELF. Penn would have approved of this. As Elias Boudinot (1740-1821), founding father, President of the Continental Congress and a U.S. Congressman from New Jersey, stated:

> Thou shalt love thy neighbor as thyself—Let it then (as workmanship of the same Divine hand) be our peculiar constant care and vigilant attention to inculcate this sacred principle, and to hand it down to posterity...Good government generally begins in the family, and if the moral character of a people once degenerate, their political character must soon follow.*

In light of the discussion offered so far, I believe that the removal of the plaque with the commandments is not constitutionally necessary, nor culturally wise, nor historically appropriate. This inappropriate solution is not neutral, but prejudicial. If having the commandments establishes a religion in the minds of some, then removing them does so in a far more emphatic manner. It does this by setting aside the "common sense" principle discussed above. Shall we next strip references of God from our monuments to Washington, Jefferson, and Lincoln, since they all refer to scripture and to God in various ways? Shall we indulge in iconoclasm in the Supreme Court Building and the Capitol Building since their iconography incorporates clear reference to the foundational roles of the Ten Commandments and the Bible for American history?[30] To do such would be to establish a secular religion based upon the nontheistic faith of free thought and the unsupportable view of the inherent goodness of man.

The Supreme Court's decision in a Texas Ten Commandments case included an important statement by now-deceased Chief Justice Rehnquist. He wrote: "Simply having religious content or promoting a message consistent with religious doctrine does not run afoul of the Establishment Clause."* The point is that while the Ten Commandments are religious, they can also have a legitimate state purpose that is consistent with the First Amendment.

So, should our courts believe that it is necessary to reflect a more pluralistic expression, then this ought to be done in a more just way than simply removing a historic plaque that commemorates the importance of The Ten Commandments for American culture. Consideration should be given to these court rulings that recognize that secular purposes are fulfilled by religious objects and documents when presented in a pluralistic expression. Thus, there is no need to remove the Ten Commandments from our courthouse walls; rather, our public places could display alongside of them other expressions of American historical values.

Simply put, whatever the separation of church and state means, it does not mean the separation of God from government!

# chapter 5

# REQUIRED HOMAGE
# TO A CREED THAT IS NOT
# ONE'S OWN

"Those who are not Jewish or Christian should not have
to pay homage to a creed that is not their own."

This raises the question of what does religious liberty mean in our culture, if it is admitted that America has had a predominantly Judeo-Christian heritage.

In responding to this important concern, I would like to review (1) America's legacy of religious liberty, (2) and America's commitment to religious liberty. Then I would like to distinguish between the (3) obligation to pay homage to a creed, and (4) the necessity of education in one's cultural heritage.

## (1) America's Legacy of Religious Liberty.

The Constitution expressly forbids religious tests for holding federal office. Many assume that this was a product of enlightenment unbelief. But the principle of religious liberty that creates this position is actually the result of our founders coming to grips with the sweeping liberty implied in the Golden Rule—"Do unto others as you would have them do unto you" (Matthew 7:12; Luke 6:31.)

This insight was initially declared by two great founders of our American colonies that became two of our original states, namely, Puritan/Baptist preacher Roger Williams and Quaker preacher William Penn. Roger Williams writes in his *Bloudy Tenent of Persecution*,

> God requireth not an uniformity of religion to be enacted and enforced in any civil state;... An enforced uniformity of religion throughout a nation or civil state confounds the civil and religious, denies the principles of Christianity and civility, and that Jesus Christ is come in the flesh.*

Williams offered three positions on religious liberty:

> That forced worship stinks in God's nostrils, that it denies Christ Jesus yet to come; and that in these flames about religion, there is no other prudent, Christian way of preserving peace in the world but by permission of differing consciences. (Sanford Cobb, *The Rise of Religious Liberty in America*, [New York: The Macmilliam Company, 1902] 427)

In a letter to the town of Providence dated January 1655, Roger Williams gave an illustration of his conception of the liberty of conscience in a commonwealth,

> There goes many a ship to sea, with many hundred souls in one ship, whose weal and woe is common, and is a true picture of a commonwealth or a human combination or society. It hath fallen out sometimes that both Papists and Protestants, Jews and Turks may be embarked in one ship; upon which supposal I affirm that all the liberty of conscience that ever I pleaded for turns upon these two hinges—that none of the papists, Protestants, Jews or Turks be forced to come to the ship's prayers or worship, nor compelled from their own particular prayers or worship, if they practice any. I further add that I never denied that, notwithstanding this liberty, the commander of this ship ought to command the ship's course, yea, and also command that justice, peace, and sobriety be kept and practiced both among the seamen and all the passengers.

William Penn in 1701 would provide his Charter of Privileges with this very first paragraph about religious liberty:

> FIRST BECAUSE noe People can be truly happy, though under the greatest Enjoyment of Civil Liberties, if abridged of the Freedom of theire Consciences, as to theire Religious Profession and Worship: And Almighty God being the only Lord of Conscience, Father of Lights and Spirits; and the Author as well as Object of all divine Knowledge, Faith and Worship, who only can Enlighten the mind, and persuade and convince the understandings of people, I doe hereby Grant and Declare, that noe person or persons, Inhabiting in

this Province or Territories, who shall Confesse and Acknowledge One Almighty God, the Creator upholder and Ruler of the World; and professe him or themselves Obliged to live quietly under the Civill Government, shall be in any Case molested or prejudiced, in his or theire Person or Estate, because of his or theire Conscientious persuasion or practice, nor be compelled to frequent or mentaine any Religious Worship place or Ministry contrary to his or theire mind or doe or suffer any other act or thing, contrary to their Religious persuasion.

This concern about religious liberty was deeply reverenced by four great founders from Virginia: George Washington, Thomas Jefferson, Patrick Henry and James Madison. Washington, as our first president, confirmed his commitment to religious freedom in his famous letter to the Jewish Congregation in Newport, Rhode Island, cited above.

Thomas Jefferson wrote the words that became the Virginia Bill for Religious Liberty:

Whereas Almighty God hath created the mind free; that all attempts to influence it by temporal punishments or burthens, or by civil incapacitations, tend only to beget habits of hypocrisy and meaness, and are a departure from the plan of the Holy author of our religion, who being Lord both of body and mind, yet chose not to propagate it by coercions on either, as was in his Almighty power to do; that the impious presumption of legislators and rulers, civil as well as ecclesiastical, who being themselves but fallible and uninspired men, have assumed dominion over the faith of others, setting up their own opinions and modes of thinking as the only true and infallible, and as such endeavouring to impose them on others, hath established and maintained false religions over the greatest part of the world, and through all time; ….Be it enacted by the General Assembly, That no man shall be compelled to frequent or support any religious worship, place or ministry whatsoever, nor shall be enforced, restrained, molested, or burthened in his body or goods, nor shall otherwise suffer on account of his religious opinions or belief; but that all men shall be free to profess, and by argument to maintain, their opinion in matters of religion, and that the same shall in no wise diminish, enlarge, or affect their civil capacities. (William R. Estep, *Revolution within the Revolution The First Amendment in the Historical Context 1612-1789* [Grand Rapids Michigan: William B. Eerdmans Publishing Company, 1990] 194-195)

Consider also Thomas Jefferson's remarkable words, "God who gave us life gave us liberty. And can the liberties of a nation be thought secure when we have removed their only firm basis, a conviction in the minds of the people that these liberties are of the Gift of God? That they are not to be violated but with His wrath? Indeed, I tremble for my country when I reflect that God is just; that His justice cannot sleep forever."[31]

*President Thomas Jefferson – "God who gave us life gave us liberty."*

Patrick Henry also had a significant impact on religious liberty in Virginia as well. In what became known as "The Parson's Cause," he helped defeat the required payment of tithes by the citizens of Virginia to the state church, a law that forced many to support a church they did not believe in. Henry also helped to defend persecuted preachers of the Gospel who were not part of the established church. William J. Federer writes,

Prior to the Revolution, in 1768, Patrick Henry rode

for miles on horseback to a trial in Spottsylvania county. He entered the rear of a courtroom where three Baptist ministers were being tried for having preached without the sanction of the Episcopalian Church. In the midst of the proceedings, he interrupted: "May it please your lordships, what did I hear read? Did I hear an expression that these men, whom you worships are about to try for misdemeanor, are charged with preaching the gospel of the Son of God?'" (In William J. Federer, *America's God and Country* [Coppel Texas: Fame Publishing, Inc., 1994] 287)

James Madison was responsible for bringing the above words by Thomas Jefferson to the Virginia State House to establish religious liberty in his home state. This reflected his deep concern for religious liberty. James Madison acknowledged and condemned the reality of religious persecution in his native Virginia in a letter to William Bradford, Jr., on January 24, 1774, calling it "that diabolical, hell-conceived principle of persecution."

Poverty and luxury prevail among all sorts; pride, ignorance, and knavery among the priesthood, and vice and wickedness among the laity. This is bad enough, but it is not the worst I have to tell you. That diabolical, hell-conceived principle of persecution rages among some; and to their eternal infamy, the clergy can furnish their quota of imps for such business. This vexes me the worst of anything whatever. There are at this time in the adjacent country not less than five or six well-meaning men in close jail for publishing their religious sentiments, which in the main are very orthodox. I have neither patience to hear, talk, or think of anything relative to this matter; for I have squabbled and scolded, abused and ridiculed, so long about it to little purpose, that I am without common

*President George W. Bush – "It is not an accident that freedom of religion is one of the central freedoms in our Bill of Rights."*

patience. So I must beg you to pity me, and pray for liberty of conscience to all. (Padover, *The Complete Madison*, p. 298.)

## (2) America's Commitment to Religious Liberty.

America's "holy experiment" has yielded religious liberty yet unknown in still half the world, which continues to face persecution marked by untold tragedy because of hostilities toward differing faith perspectives. Sadly, much of the world still does not enjoy the religious freedom that Americans experience on a daily basis. In a speech by President George W. Bush, given on May 7, 2001 to the American Jewish Committee entitled, "The First Freedom of the Soul," President Bush underscored the profound need for religious liberty worldwide:

> The Middle East is the birthplace of three great religions: Judaism, Christianity, and Islam. Lasting peace in the region must respect the rights of believers in all these faiths. That's common sense. But it is also something more: it is moral sense, based upon the deep American commitment to freedom of religion...
>
> Leo Napoleon Levi, a Galveston, Texas, lawyer and a president of the national B'nai Brith, drafted President Theodore Roosevelt a telegram denouncing a Russian pogrom in 1903. The Czar of Russia was so stung by Roosevelt's message that he formally refused to accept it. Some Americans complained that Roosevelt had gone too far. He replied that there were crimes so monstrous that the American conscience had to assert itself. And there still are.

No one is a better witness to the transience of tyranny than the children of Abraham. Forty centuries ago, the Jewish people were entrusted with a truth more enduring than any power of man. In the words of the prophet Isaiah, "This shall be My covenant with them, said the Lord; My spirit which is upon you, and the words which I have placed in your mouth, shall not be absent from your mouth, nor from the mouth of your children, nor from the mouth of your children's children – said the Lord-from now, for all time..."

It is not an accident that freedom of religion is one of the central freedoms in our Bill of Rights. It is the first freedom of the human soul: the right to speak the words that God places in our mouths. We must stand for that freedom in our country. We must speak for that freedom in the world.

The President detailed in his speech all the areas in the world where crimes against humanity are being committed in the name of religious faith. There are indeed "crimes so monstrous that the American conscience has to assert itself." Clearly, liberty's message still needs to be heard throughout the hurting, hungry, and poverty stricken nations of the world. Isn't it palpably ironic that we are troubled in America about pledging our allegiance to the flag of "one nation under God," whose very views of God and government have been the world's first real hope for religious liberty?!

### (3) Is there an obligation to pay homage to a creed that is not one's own?

The point you raise here was addressed in the federal

*The Islamic Society of Northern Wisconsin*

92

courtroom where I had the privilege to testify on behalf of keeping the Ten Commandments on the wall in West Chester, Chester County, Pennsylvania. It especially arose in regard to the presence of many Muslims in America. Thus, Professor Blankinship from Temple University in Philadelphia presented expert testimony on behalf of the position that sought to remove the Ten Commandments. He is correct when he writes in his paper for the court, "There is no question that

*Bible passage from Leviticus 25:10 inscribed on the Liberty Bell (shown is The Providence Forum's replica of the Liberty Bell)*

the Muslims in the United States are an important part of the religious and cultural scene that cannot be ignored. Their existence here represents an increase in the religious pluralism here that was formerly confined to the Christian and Jewish traditions, but now includes many others."* To this important observation, and as an excellent example for addressing "those who are not Jewish or Christian" as you mention in your letter, allow me to make the following observations.

While there is no "religious" continuity between Islam and the Ten Commandments, there is moral continuity between them. The moral perspective of Islam rejects the Bible. Yet the Muslim moral teachings are in substance the same with the commandments that are found in the Bible. This moral commonality is significant for the question before us. The posting of the commandments is not for explicitly religious purposes, that is, to establish a religion. Rather they are displayed for the "secular" intent of advancing the morality that is necessary for our republican forms of government to flourish. Thus, even with respect to the American Muslim minority, our founders' appeal to the commandments to sustain good government is both relevant and yet mindful of First Amendment concerns. The display of the commandments serves to uphold a common moral community life necessary for the government of all citizens, yet it does not establish the state sanctioned religion.

Muslims have begun to seek to enter into the American political culture, and thus, Professor Blankinship writes, "Muslims who have grown up here and who know the structure of the political system and thus know their rights may well doubt the wisdom of the public display of a text that their religion does not acknowledge and which, indeed, is the primary property of another competing religion. That would seem to be unfair competition and contrary to the principles of equality under the law."* This statement is profoundly important for responding to the Muslim presence in America. Muslims appropriately seek their rights afforded by the governmental application of the Judeo-Christian ideal of religious liberty even for minorities.[32] However, does Islam, at this precise point find continuity with the American tradition of "liberty in law" which is afforded by the commandments that are displayed on the wall of the West Chester Courthouse?[32] It is the Judeo-Christian Torah

*Ground Zero after September 11, 2001*

text of Leviticus 25:10, rejected as potentially "corrupted," according to Muslim teaching that is on the Liberty Bell. This great symbol of American religious and civil liberty declares: "Proclaim Liberty throughout all the land unto all the inhabitants thereof."[33]

I regard the tragic terrorist assaults of September 11, 2001, as an aberrant form of Islamic jihad warfare against American culture. I hope this to be true.[34] But even more normative Muslim countries have been characterized as some of the least free in the world.[35]

94

Speaking of the worldwide growth of Islam, Professor Blankinship explains, "It has also become the majority religion of many countries, including Morocco, Algeria, Tunisia, Libya, Egypt, the Sudan, Mauritania, Senegal, Gambia, Guinea, Mali, Niger, Chad, Nigeria, Eritrea, Djibouti, Somalia, Saudi Arabia, Yemen, Oman, the United Arab Emirates, Qatar, Bahrain, Kuwait, the Palestinian entity, Jordan, Lebanon, Turkey, Albania, Syria, Iraq, Iran, Azerbaijan, Uzbekistan, Tajikistan, Turkmenistan, Kygystan, Afghanistan, Pakistan, Bangladesh, Malaysia, Brunei, Indonesia, the Maldives Islands, and the Comoro Islands."* Significantly, most of these countries either do not possess or significantly restrict religious freedom, according to the United States' State Department.[36] Most have experienced religious persecution in the name of Islam. This is what occurs when Judeo-Christian principles are undermined.

Professor Blankinship states that it is unfortunate that it has been said "that Muslims do not integrate well into our political system here because they deny its legitimacy." Muslim leaders should answer a critical question: Does the Qur'an require Muslims to deny the legitimacy of the American system of religious and civil liberty? This is a fundamental question for the health of American constitutional liberty. Do Muslims affirm the legitimacy of the First Amendment, even for Muslims who may seek to leave their faith, and for other religions to seek to convert Muslims to their views? These concerns are relevant for "nontheistic" freethinkers as well, who desire freedom to persuade others to their point of view. The First Amendment establishes these rights. Will a Muslim ascendancy in America seek to perpetuate this tradition of liberty in law that has emerged from the Judeo-Christian tradition, as reflected in the commandments on the wall of the West Chester Courthouse? These issues give additional impetus for the state's interest in maintaining the commandments, where an earlier generation chose not just to place them, but to commemorate them.

Thus, ironically, it is the nonestablishment of religion that developed from America's Judeo-Christian heritage of liberty that enables the very pluralistic religious life referred to by Professor Blankinship: "Adherents of other religions, such as Hindus, Buddhists, Taoists, Confucianists, and Shintoists, not to mention followers of non-Christian American Indian traditions or Wiccans, are all the more left out, because none of their religions acknowledges the Bible as a scripture nor any of its personages as religious figures at all.

Followers of all of these religions will tend to feel excluded by the display of this text on a public building that belongs to all citizens."* The point is this, the civil religion enshrined in the American tradition has a secular common sense purpose of protecting religious liberty and the survival of republican government. This civil religion of America flowing from the commandments enables these minority religions to prosper in America. The commandments themselves are thus the progenitors of our Bill of Rights and the religious liberty afforded in the First Amendment. Would these various religions prosper under Islamic law? Would they flourish under any law system that did not value freedom as the Judeo-Christian tradition has? Religious liberty was discovered and perfected by the Christian colonists of America, and so far, it has substantially impacted only half of the world.[38]

Professor Blankinship argues that there is an offensive character of the commandments toward Catholics by their display on the wall of the West Chester Courthouse: "The plaque in question uses the King James translation of the Bible, which is not acceptable to all Christians. Most Protestants, perhaps, like the Protestant clergy who participated in the original installation of the plaque, would not particularly disapprove of such an artifact, even if they no longer use that translation. But the translation does exclude the Roman Catholics, who have never used that rendition and have always had their own translations. Likewise, the Jews have their own biblical translations and interpretations."* In response, I would note the following telling remarks of Father Meehan, also a witness in the case, as well as a remark by Orthodox Rabbi Daniel Lapin. Father Francis X. Meehan writes,

> Regarding the listing of commandments on the Chester County courthouse, I would like to state the following.
>
> As a Roman Catholic, as a parish priest, and as a former professor of theology at St. Charles Seminary, I wish to state that I have absolutely no theological problem with the listing of the Commandments, or with the translation of those Commandments, as they are so listed on the Courthouse.
>
> I have been asked if, in any way, the particular

translation, namely the King James Version, is offensive to Roman Catholics. The answer is, unequivocally, no. At no time in my 40 years as a priest, have I ever heard that the King James Version of the Commandments offers any offense to Roman Catholics. I have never heard nor can I think of any reason to have any theological objection to this translation of the commandments as they appear on the Chester County Courthouse or anywhere else. (Letter to Thomas C. Abrahamsen, Ass't County Solicitor, The County of Chester, dated February 10, 2002.)

Orthodox Rabbi Daniel Lapin writes,

Why do the descendants of the people who gave the world the Ten Commandments seem more hostile to them than anyone else in America? . . .After a great deal of thought and years spent in detailed analyses of countless ancient Jewish texts that predict this trend in my people, the following is my answer. To understand this phenomenon, one has to know that Jewish attraction to liberalism is not new. In one form or another, many Jews have been liberals for more than three thousand years. Talmudic tradition reports that upon receiving the Ten Commandments, the Israelites wept. Their gloom was caused by the realization that the godly revelation they had just experienced now prohibited the lascivious lifestyle to which they had grown accustomed in Egypt. At that moment, liberalism was born: the eternal search for liberation from God's seemingly restrictive rules. There are those who will always seek—or if necessary, create—the escape hatch through which those who find God's rules too limiting can flee. (Rabbi Daniel Lapin,

*America's Real War: An Orthodox Rabbi Insists that*
*Judeo-Christian Values Are Vital For Our Nation's*
*Survival,* 269)

Differences in the presentation of the commandments, however, do not necessarily imply distinction in substance. These differences between the traditions are a living strength of the American pluralism in religion that has made our nation the most free among all of the nations on earth.

While history and tradition are important, I agree that the legitimate rights of each viewpoint must be measured. Yet coupled with these concerns is the profoundly practical concern of the need to protect our culture from anarchy, violence, hate-crimes, terrorism, mass murders (such as are reflected in the Columbine shootings), and the destruction of the World Trade Center, the Pentagon and the government office building in Oklahoma City. There is a compelling and continuing cultural relevance for learning the commandments.

Moreover, removing the commandments silences the voice of our nation's history and tradition, both past as well as in its living expression. The plaque, as has been noted, is an ecumenical and eclectic expression of the moral values of our heritage. Even those expert witnesses, who oppose its presence, admit that its values reflect in some measure the Jewish, Christian, and Muslim faiths.

The point here, then, is not to compel anyone to pay homage to a creed that is not their own. Rather, it is to recognize that the very fabric of American democracy contains certain values that all Americans must hold. If they hold them because they are contained in the Ten Commandments, that is fine. If they hold them because they believe they simply are wise, that is fine. The issue is not the establishment of religion, but the establishment of religious liberty in a society of order and justice.

**(4) The necessity of education in one's cultural heritage.**
There is a dictum attributed to Marx that says, "Take away a people's roots, and they can easily be moved." One of our great national dangers is ignorance of America's profound legacy of freedom.

I firmly believe that ignorance is a threat to freedom. And sadly, there are many signs of America's ignorance about its own heritage. Our country started in Philadelphia, but if The Providence Forum had not stepped forward in 2001, the triple anniversaries of 300 years of religious liberty, the 250th anniversary of the ordering of the Liberty Bell, and the 225th anniversary of America's independence would have been mostly overlooked. Why was Philadelphia the second largest English-speaking city in the world, when it was only seventy-five years old, and 3,000 miles away from London, across a vast ocean? The answer is religious liberty. Philadelphia in 2001 had almost completely forgotten that its city had grown because of William Penn's guarantee of religious liberty as declared in his Charter of Privileges which, as noted below, stated that:

*Karl Marx – "Take away a people's roots, and they can easily be moved."*

> noe person or persons, Inhabiting in this Province or Territories, who shall Confesse and Acknowledge One Almighty God, the Creator upholder and Ruler of the World; and professe him or themselves Obliged to live quietly under the Civill Government, shall be in any Case molested or prejudiced, in his or theire Person or Estate, because of his or theire Conscientious persuasion or practice, nor be compelled to frequent or mentaine any Religious Worship place or Ministry contrary to his or theire mind or doe or suffer any other act or thing, contrary to their Religious persuasion.

Similarly, here in Philadelphia, at the home of the American Flag, the location of the home of Betsy Ross, we nearly forgot the American Flag's 225th anniversary.

The importance of all of our citizens knowing our nation's heritage is so that we can truly be free. Consider these thoughts by our founders about the interconnection of education and liberty:

Thomas Jefferson:
A nation has never been ignorant and free; that has never been and will never be.*

James Madison:
Learned institutions ought to be favorite objects with every free people. They throw that light over the public mind which is the best security against crafty and dangerous encroachments on the public liberty. (To W. T. Barry, August 4, 1822. In *The Complete Madison: His Basic Writings*, ed. Saul K. Padover, [New York: Harper & Brothers, 1953], 337)

The diffusion of knowledge is the only guardian of true liberty. (James Madison to George Thompson, June 30, 1825)

It is universally admitted that a well-instructed people alone can be permanently a free people. (James Madison, *Second Annual Message*, December 5, 1810)

Samuel Adams:
Let divines and philosophers, statesmen and patriots, unite their endeavors to renovate the age, by impressing the minds of men with the importance of educating their little boys and girls, of inculcating in the minds of youth the fear and love of the Deity and universal philanthropy, and, in subordination to these great principles, the love of their country; of instructing them in the art of self-government, without which they never can act a wise part in the government of societies, great or small; in short, of leading them in the study and practice of the exalted virtues of the Christian system.*

In corroboration of this point, I cite a speaker that I heard recently who described this historical ignorance of Americans of our heritage by the provocative phrase, "American amnesia." Is that an overstatement? If you think so, consider these statistics that he offered:

Nearly half of incoming students to several of our premier universities could not state the Emancipation Proclamation's half century.

Nearly 80 percent of seniors at fifty-five top colleges and universities, including Harvard and Princeton received a D or F on a thirty-four question, high school level American History test. Questions included "Are the words Give me Liberty or give me death' familiar to you?" and "Do you think Thomas Jefferson was the 'Father of the Constitution'?" Only 23 percent identified James Madison as the true "Father of the Constitution." George Washington is on his way to being eliminated from elementary school textbooks!

Nearly half of incoming students to several of these same schools thought that the words "Take from those with much and give to those with less" were found in the U.S. Constitution! They didn't know that it was from Karl Marx!

Unfortunately, these facts, coupled with the well-recognized and oft described "moral decay" of America illustrate Marx's maxim: "Take away a people's roots, and they can easily be moved."

## (5) A review of some of America's history that demonstrates the impact of religious beliefs on our nation's identity.

A true education in the American cultural context will provide a true rendition of America's history, its values and beliefs that helped to forge the

*Christopher Columbus – "No one should fear to undertake a task in the name of our Savior."*

institutions that govern our lives today. American freedom is clearly a product of the Judeo-Christian heritage.[39] Some of our founders argued for the importance of the Bible in public education.[40] We can see Christian influence in our early nation's calls for prayer. This can be seen also in many of the writings of our first president, George Washington. Rather than being a deist, as is so often alleged, he affirms his belief in providence,[41] and he repeatedly expresses himself with clear Christian commitment.[42] The importance of the Bible for our national leaders has been indicated time and again in their public statements.[43]

Consider the remarkable historical insights that we gain about our nation when we consider the following historical facts, even if we disagree with the faith that they express:

The excerpts from the diary of Christopher Columbus, relating to his motivation to embark on the dangerous journey which opened the New World say:

> It was the Lord who put it into my mind—I could feel His hand upon me—the fact that it would be possible to sail from here to the Indies...
>
> All who heard of my project rejected it with laughter, ridiculing me... There is no question that the inspiration was from the Holy Spirit, because He comforted me with rays of marvelous illumination from the Holy Scriptures... For the execution of the journey to the Indies, I did not make use of intelligence, mathematics, or maps. It is simply the fulfillment of what Isaiah had prophesied....
>
> No one should fear to undertake a task in the name of our Savior, if it is just and if the intention is purely for His Service.... The fact that the Gospel must still be preached to so many lands in such a short time—this is what convinces me.

The Pilgrims' Mayflower Compact showing the first written

*The signing of the Mayflower Compact*

constitutional government of free men:

> In ye name of God, Amen. We whose names are underwritten, the loyall subjects of our dread soveraigne Lord, King James, by ye grace of God, of Great Britaine, France, & Ireland king, defender of ye faith, &c., haveing undertaken, for ye glorie of God, and advancemente of ye Christian faith, and honour of our king & countrie, a voyage to plant ye first colonie in ye Northerne parts of Virginia, doe by these presents solemnly & mutually in ye presence of God, and one of another, covenant & combine our selves togeather into a civill body politick, for our better ordering & preservation & furtherance of ye ends aforesaid; and by vertue hearof to enacte, constitute, and frame such just & equall lawes, ordinances, acts, constitutions, & offices, from time to time, as shall be thought most meete & convenient for ye generall good of ye Colonie, unto which we promise all due submission

and obedience.

America's First Education Act: The Old Deluder Law of 1647 established the first free common schools in America. The legislature of Massachusetts enacted a law with the following preamble:

> It being one chief purpose of that old deluder, Satan, to keep men from the knowledge of the Scripture, it was therefore ordered that every township containing fifty families or householders should set up a school in which children might be taught to read and write, and that every township containing one hundred families or householders should set up a school in which boys might be fitted for entering Harvard College. (APH, p. 104)

The Mottoes and Purpose Statements of America's Premier Colleges:

> 1. Harvard University Motto:
> *"For Christ and the Church"* est. By Rev. John Harvard
> Purpose for Harvard's establishment as published in "New England's First Fruits" in 1643:
> After God had carried us safe to New England, and wee had builded our houses, provided necessaries for our liveli-hood, rear'd convenient places for Gods worship, and settled the Civil Government: One of the next things we longed for, and looked after was to advance Learning, and perpetuate it to Posterity, dreading to leave an illiterate Ministry to the Churches, when our present Ministers shall lie in the Dust. (APH p. 109)

> Rules and Precepts observed in the College:
> Let every student be plainly instructed, and earnestly pressed to consider well, the maine end of his life and studies is, to know God and Jesus Christ which is eternall life, (John 17:3), and therefore to lay Christ in the bottome, as the only

foundation of all sound knowledge and Learning. (Ibid. pp. 109-110)

2. *College of William and Mary* (Charter via Rev. James Blair) to the end that the Church of Virginia may be furnished with a seminary of ministers of the gospel and...that the Christian faith may be propagated...to the glory of God (APH, p. 111)

3. *Yale University* (Official charter, 1701) for the liberal and religious education of suitable youth...to propagate in this wilderness, the blessed reformed Protestant religion (APH p. 111)

4. *Princeton University*
First President, Rev. Jonathan Dickinson
Cursed be all that learning that is contrary to the cross of Christ.
Official Motto: Under God's Power She Flourishes (APH, p.111)

5. *Rutgers University*
Official Motto: Son of Righteousness, Shine upon the West also (APH, p.111)

## The Importance of the Bible for many of our nation's leaders

America's presidents and patriots have often stated the centrality and necessity of the Bible for our form of government. As George Washington said,

> The foundation of our Empire was not laid in the gloomy age of Ignorance and Superstition, but at an Epocha when the rights of mankind were better understood and more clearly defined, than at any former period, the researches of the human mind, after social happiness, have been carried to a great

extent, the Treasures of knowledge, acquired by the labours of Philosophers, Sages and Legislature, through a long succession of years, are laid open for our use, and their collected wisdom may be happily applied in the Establishment of our forms of Government; the free cultivation of Letters, the unbounded extension of Commerce, the progressive refinement of Manners, the growing liberality of sentiment *and above all, the pure and benign light of Revelation,* have had a meliorating influence on mankind and increased the blessings of Society.* (emphasis mine.)

Patrick Henry said,

The Bible is worth all other books which have ever been printed.[44]

In 1844, the U.S. Supreme Court told a Philadelphia school:

Why may not the Bible, and especially the New Testament...be read and taught as a divine revelation in the [school]—its general precepts expounded... and its glorious principles of morality inculcated?... Where can the purest principles of morality be learned so clearly or so perfectly as from the New Testament.*

Andrew Jackson said on June 8, 1845,

That book, Sir, is the Rock upon which our republic rests.

President Woodrow Wilson said,

There are a good many problems before the

American people today, and before me as President, but I expect to find the solution to those problems just in the proportion that I am faithful in the study of the Word of God.*

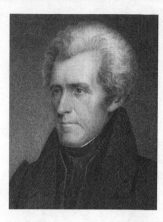

President Andrew Jackson – "That book, Sir, is the rock upon which our republic rests."

How ironic that the book that was President Wilson's source of the solutions for the problems of America is now exiled from the schools of our land that are overflowing with problems!

Consider again Congress' proclamation of 1983 as the Year of the Bible, cited previously. In light of all the above, when our public schools fail to include an honest representation of our nation's history, that embraces such deep spiritual interest, are they not committing an enormous, intellectual error of omission? Doesn't such anti-religious selectivity actually belie a deeper effort to suppress or censor a substantive part of America's intellectual heritage? Why should we be afraid to teach our nation's historical faith, even if many freely choose not to believe it today?

The sad conclusion that I must reach is that the educational model of our public schools and many of the recent rulings of our federal courts make it abundantly clear that America's traditional and generous "common sense perspective" concerning religious liberty and the free exercise of religion, discussed above, has been abandoned. Thankfully, Supreme Court rulings may be beginning to correct this. See, for example, Kenneth Starr's book, *First Among Equals,* where he discusses the High Court's attempts to protect freedom of speech in regard to religious matters in public places (p. 58-69).

The point that must be underscored is that America truly is the home of religious liberty. No one here is forced to pay homage to a creed that is not his own! This reality is one of the greatest gifts of the Judeo-Christian heritage to the world. The national history that produced such liberty ought to be well known by all its citizens, even if not all of these citizens agree with the religious influences that helped to shape this liberty.

# chapter 6

# TAX DOLLARS
# AND FAITH-BASED
# MINISTRIES

"Neither should they have to support our mission with their tax dollars."

Your comment raises the question of should the government in any way provide financial support for faith-based programs, given the fact that not all citizens operate from a vantage point of faith.

As America reconsiders the value of faith-based organizations for the meeting of social needs, many question if this new faith emphasis is consistent with our nation's understanding of the distinction between church and state. Concerned citizens on both sides of the "wall" will undoubtedly attempt to calculate how high and impregnable a "wall of separation between church and state" ought to be. To love one's neighbor as oneself is both social and religious. To respect just laws toward God and man is both religious and social.

## (1) The value of faith-based initiatives in assisting the government in addressing social problems

But whatever dimensions of Thomas Jefferson's metaphorical wall you feel are necessary in our pluralistic society, I believe that the church's faith in God and the state's concern to rectify societal problems are not inherently contradictory. This is because God's providence acts not only in the hearts of people, but also in the history of governments. Moreover, the societal problems that concern the state are, in their essence, issues of the heart and therefore the domain of true religion also.

I am sure you are aware of the famous quotation attributed to Alexis De Tocqueville summarizing his analysis of the early years of America:

> I sought for the key to the greatness and genius of America in her harbors...; in her fertile fields and boundless forests; in her rich mines and vast world commerce; in her public school system and institutions of learning. I sought for it in her democratic Congress and in her matchless Constitution. Not until I went into the churches of America and heard her pulpits flame with righteousness did I understand the secret of her genius and power. America is great because America is good, and if America ever ceases to be good, America will cease to be great.[45]

Inasmuch as I agree with de Tocqueville, I, for one, am grateful for both the Clinton and Bush administrations' interest in and support of faith-based and faith-motivated initiatives. In essence, this movement has simply rediscovered de Tocqueville's insight. Scholars researching the urban social milieu are focusing anew on the churches of our land—what de Tocqueville deemed the "secret of America's genius and power." A *Wall Street Journal* article declares, "Especially in America's high-crime, low-literacy neighborhoods, organized religion remains the backbone of civil society."[46]

I hope you have been able to follow some of the recent actions of President Bush. One of substantial significance for our discussion here occurred on December 12, 2002, when President Bush signed an executive order in Philadelphia entitled, "Equal Protection of the Laws for Faith-Based and Community Organizations." Some of his remarks address your concern about "tax dollars" being paid to support the mission of a faith-based organization whose faith one cannot conscientiously support. President Bush's words are powerful:

> Many faiths and many traditions are represented here. Yet we share the same belief that every person in need is a worthy child of God. And we share the same goal: We must bring the hope and healing of faith-based services to more and more Americans.
>
> Government has often been slow to recognize the importance of faith-based and community efforts. That's changing. And more changes are needed.
>
> No government policy can put hope in people's hearts or a sense of purpose in people's lives. That is done when someone, some good soul puts an arm around a neighbor and says, God loves you, and I love, and you can count on us both.
>
> Faith-based charities work daily miracles because they have idealistic volunteers. They're guided by moral principles. They know the problems of their own communities, and above all, they recognize the dignity of every citizen and the

possibilities of every life. These groups and many good charities that are specifically religious have the heart to serve others. Yet many lack the resources they need to meet the needs around them.

They deserve the support of the rest of us. They deserve the support of foundations. They deserve the support of corporate America. They deserve the support of individual donors, of church congregations, of synagogues and mosques. And they deserve, when appropriate, the support of the federal government.

Faith-based groups will never replace government when it comes to helping those in need. Yet government must recognize the power and unique contribution of faith-based groups in every part of our country. And when the federal government gives contracts to private groups to provide social services, religious groups should have an equal chance to compete. When decisions are made on public funding, we should not focus on the religion you practice; we should focus on the results you deliver.

Throughout his speech I find it ironic that the president agrees with you in being very concerned about discrimination, but the object of discrimination he identifies is quite different from the one you identify! He sees people of faith as a whole being discriminated against by government agencies, while you are concerned that a specific religious group will be singled out by the government for discrimination.

So today, I'm announcing a series of actions to stop the unfair treatment of religious charities by the federal government. If a charity is helping the needy, it should not matter if there is a rabbi on the board, or a cross or a crescent on the wall, or a religious commitment in the charter. The days of discriminating against religious groups just because they are religious are coming to an end.

These are examples of a larger pattern, a pattern of discrimination. And this discrimination shows a fundamental misunderstanding of the law.

When government discriminates against religious groups, it is not the groups that suffer most. The loss comes to the hungry who don't get fed, to the addicts who don't get help, to the children who drift toward self-destruction. For the sake of so many brothers and sisters in need, we must and we will support the armies of compassion in America.

In acting to correct the flagrant discrimination against faith-based groups by the government, the president also agrees with you that no people of faith should be forced to change their faith to work with government, or to have their tax dollars go to support a faith they do not accept.

I recognize that government has no business endorsing a religious creed, or directly funding religious worship or religious teaching. That is not the business of the government. Yet, government can and should support social services provided by religious people, as long as those services go to anyone in need, regardless of their faith. And when government gives that support, charities and faith-based programs would not be forced to change their character or compromise their mission.

Through all these actions, I hope that every faith-based group in America, the social entrepreneurs of America, understand that this government respects your work and we respect the motivation behind your work. We do not want you to become carbon copies of public programs. We want you to follow your heart. We want you to follow the word. We want you to do the works of kindness and mercy you are called upon to do.

And in his striking this balance, also note that the president believes that faith in God does have a place in government.

> For too long, for too long, some in government believed there was no room for faith in the public square. I guess they've forgotten the history of this great country. People of faith led the struggle against slavery. People of faith fought against child labor. People of faith worked for women's equality and civil rights. Every expansion of justice in American history received inspiration from men and women of moral conviction and religious belief.. And in America today, people of faith are waging a determined campaign against need and suffering.

I believe that President Bush has here rediscovered and is modeling the common sense pluralism described by our nation's founders and defined by our earlier courts: "We are a religious people, and our institutions presuppose a Supreme Being."

## (2) Past presidential recognition of the power of faith to improve societal ills

In concluding this section, consider a speech by an earlier American president, Calvin Coolidge, wherein he expresses his appreciation for the contribution of a great religious worker for the building of American civilization. Thus, on October 15, 1924, at the unveiling of the Equestrian Statue of Methodist Bishop Francis Asbury, Washington, D.C., President Calvin Coolidge stated:

> As we review their accomplishments, they constantly admonish us not only that "all things work together for good to them that love God," but that in the direction of the affairs of our country there has been an influence that had a broader

*President Calvin Coolidge – "Our government rests upon religion."*

vision, greater wisdom and a wider purpose than that of mortal man, which we can only ascribe to a Divine Providence.

To one of them, Francis Asbury, the first American bishop of the Methodist Episcopal Church, and his associates, made a tremendous contribution. Our government rests upon religion. It is from that source that we derive our reverence for truth and justice, for equality and liberty, and for the rights of mankind. Unless the people believe in these principles, they cannot believe in our government. There are only two main theories of government in the world. One rests on righteousness, the other rests on force. One appeals to reason, the other appeals to the sword. One is exemplified in a republic; the other is represented by a despotism. The history of government on this earth has been almost entirely a history of the rule of force held in the hands of a few. Under our Constitution America committed itself to the practical application of the rule of reason, with the power in the hands of the people.

It is of a great deal of significance that the generation which fought the American Revolution had seen a very extensive religious revival. They had heard the preaching of Jonathan Edwards. They had seen the great revival meetings that were inspired also by the preaching of Whitefield. The religious experiences of those days made a profound impression upon the great body of the people. They made new thoughts and created new interests. They freed the public mind, through a deeper knowledge and more serious contemplation of the truth. By calling the people to righteousness they were a direct preparation for self-government. It was for a continuation of this work that Francis Asbury was raised up.

The religious movement which he represented was distinctly a movement to reach the great body of the people. Just as our Declaration of Independence asserts that all men are created free, so it seems to me the founders of this movement were inspired by the thought that all men were worthy to hear the Word, worthy to be sought out and brought to salvation. It was this motive that took their preachers among the poor and neglected, even to criminals in the jails. As our ideal has been to bring all men to freedom, so their ideal was to bring all men to salvation.

Just as the time was approaching when our country was about to begin the work of establishing a government which was to represent the rule of the people, where not a few but the many were to control public affairs, where the vote of the humblest was to count for as much as the most exalted, Francis Asbury came to America to preach religion.

He was the son of a father who earned his livelihood by manual labor, of a mother who bore a reputation for piety. By constant effort they provided the ordinary comforts of life and an opportunity for intellectual and religious instruction. It was thus that he came out of a home of the people. Very early, at the age of seventeen, he began his preaching. In 1771, when he was twenty-six years old, responding to a call for volunteers, he was sent by Wesley to America. Landing in Philadelphia, he began that ministry which in the next forty-five years was to take him virtually all through the colonies and their western confines and into Canada, from Maine on the north, almost to the Gulf of Mexico on the south.

He came to America five years after the formation of the first Methodist Society in the city of New York, which had been contemporaneous with his own joining of the British Conference as an itinerant preacher and a gospel missionary. At that time it is reported that there were 316 members of his denomination in this country. The prodigious character of his labors is revealed when we remember that he traveled some 6,000 miles each year, or in all about 270,000 miles, preaching about 15,500 sermons and ordaining more than 4,000 clergymen, besides presiding at no less than 224 Annual Conferences. The highest salary that he received was $80 each year for this kind of service, which meant exposure to summer heat and winter cold, traveling alone through the frontier forests, sharing the rough fare of the pioneer's cabin, until his worn-out frame was laid at last to rest. But he left behind him as one evidence of his labors 695 preachers and 214,235 members of his denomination. The vitality of the cause which he served is further revealed by recalling that the 316 with which he began has now grown to more than 800,000.

His problem during the Revolutionary War was that of continuing to perform his duties without undertaking to interfere in civil or military affairs. He had taken for the text of his first sermon in America these very significant words: "For I determined not to know anything among you save Jesus Christ and Him crucified." When several of his associates left for England in 1775, he decided to stay. "I can by no means agree to leave such a field for gathering souls to Christ as we have in America," he writes, "therefore I am determined by the grace of God not to leave them, let the consequence by what it may...."

He had no lack of loyalty to the early form of American government. When the inauguration of Washington took place April 30, 1789, the Conference being in session, Bishop Asbury moved the presentation of a congratulatory address to the new President. His suggestion was adopted, and the Bishop being one of those designated for the purpose, presenting the address in person, read it to Washington.

How well he fitted into the scheme of things, this circuit rider who spent his life making stronger the foundation on which our government rests and seeking to implant in the hearts of all men, however poor and unworthy they may have seemed, an increased ability to discharge the high duties of their citizenship. His outposts marched with the pioneers; his missionaries visited the hovels of the poor so that all men might be brought to a knowledge of the truth.

A great lesson has been taught us by this holy life. It was because of what Bishop Asbury and his associates preached and what other religious organizations, through their ministry, preached that our country has developed so much freedom and contributed so much to the civilization of the world.

The government of a country never gets ahead of the religion of a country. There is no way by which we can substitute the authority of law for the virtue of man.... Real reforms which society in these days is seeking will come as a result of our religious convictions, or they will not come at all. Peace, justice, humanity, charity — these cannot be legislated into being. They are the result of a Divine Grace.

How many homes he must have hallowed! What a multitude of frontier mothers must have brought their children to him to receive his blessings! It is more than probable that Nancy Hanks, the mother of Lincoln, had heard him in her youth. Adams and Jefferson must have known him, and Jackson must have seen in him a flaming spirit as unconquerable as his own. How many temples of worship dot our landscape; how many institutions of learning, some of them rejoicing in the name Wesleyan, all trace the inspiration of their existence to the sacrifice and service of this lone circuit rider. He is entitled to rank as one of the builders of our nation.

On the foundation of a religious civilization which he sought to build, our country has enjoyed greater blessing of liberty and prosperity than was ever before the lot of man. These cannot continue if we neglect the work which he did. We cannot depend on the government to do the work of religion. I do not see how anyone could recount the story of this early Bishop without feeling a renewed faith in our own country.[47]

The point I wish to make here is that faith-based initiatives call for a new generation of circuit riders to minister "among the poor and neglected, even to criminals in the jails. As our ideal has been to bring all men to freedom. . . ." Can't we agree with President Coolidge's concluding words? They are worth repeating because of the important point they make:

On the foundation of a religious civilization which he sought to build, our country has enjoyed greater blessing of liberty and prosperity than was ever before the lot of man. These cannot continue if we

> neglect the work which he did. We cannot depend
> on the government to do the work of religion. I do
> not see how anyone could recount the story of this
> early Bishop without feeling a renewed faith in our
> own country.

Notice well President Coolidge's intimate connection between "religious civilization" and the "greater blessing of liberty and prosperity than was ever before the lot of man."

Once Alexis de Tocqueville observed, "Christianity, therefore reigns [in America] without obstacle, by universal consent; the consequence is, as I have before observed, that every principle of the moral world is fixed and determinate..."* Certainly then, Tocqueville and Coolidge would not have understood President Bush's trilogy of "church congregations, synagogues and mosques." While we are no longer monolithically a Christian culture, the important point to note here is that we must maintain a constant commitment to the historic and effective moral underpinnings of our free society, and the concomitant important role of religion in the welfare of our national identity. An authentic pluralism will respect and encourage the legitimate role of religious diversity in public life.

# chapter 7

# THE INTEGRITY OF THE GOSPEL IN GOVERNMENT DRESS

"In order for the government to promote Judeo-Christian values without trampling on the rights of non-Jews and non-Christians, those values have to be watered down to the point that they have very little to do with the gospel of Jesus Christ."

Your comment raises another excellent question.

**(1) Does a constitutionally required governmental neutrality toward religion inevitably corrupt authentic Christian faith as soon as the government seeks a way to be involved?**

The necessity of a national religious culture or worldview, by definition, is not intended to be the same as religion itself. While we are not accustomed these days to speak of a "public religion" or a "cultural religion," our founders understood that culture is inherently religious because it established our general norms or values. This was, for example, clearly evident in the speech I quoted at the conclusion of the last section by President Calvin Coolidge. In fact, Benjamin Franklin made this point in 1749 in his proposal for the University of Pennsylvania, where he speaks of the necessity of a "Publick Religion."

> History will also afford frequent Opportunities of showing the Necessity of a Publick Religion, from its Usefulness to the Publick; the Advantage of a Religious Character among private Persons; the Mischiefs of Superstition, etc. and the Excellency of the Christian Religion above all others ancient or modern.

Franklin's point is motivated by pragmatic realities of culture. Notice his words, "usefulness, advantage, excellency." The point is that somebody's, some religion's, some philosophy's values will always permeate culture. The question is not whether this will be so, but which of these system's values will have cultural hegemony. Culture is never neutral.

What Franklin called "a publick religion," we might better call a worldview. In a 1933 lecture called "The Question of a Weltanschauung," Sigmund Freud defined a worldview as "an intellectual construction which solves all the problems of our existence uniformly on the basis of one overriding hypothesis." Alexis de Tocqueville wrote in 1838 in his *Democracy in America*,

> It is therefore of immense importance to men to have fixed ideas about God, their soul, and their

duties toward their Creator and their fellows, for doubt about these first principles would leave all their actions to chance and condemn them, more or less, to anarchy and impotence.

This is what President Theodore Roosevelt was getting at when he spoke several years later in 1909 regarding a "Christian Civilization"

Progress has brought us both unbounded opportunities and unbridled difficulties. Thus, the measure of our civilization will not be that we have done much, but what we have done with that much. I believe that the next half century will determine if we will advance the cause of Christian civilization or revert to the horrors of brutal paganism. The thought of modern industry in the hands of Christian charity is a dream worth dreaming. The thought of industry in the hands of paganism is a nightmare beyond imagining. The choice between the two is upon us.*

Dr. Armand Nicholi, professor of psychiatry at Harvard, explains it this way,

All of us, whether we realize it or not, have a worldview; we have a philosophy of life —our attempt to make sense of our existence. It contains our answers to the fundamental questions concerning the meaning of our lives, questions that we struggle with at some level all of our lives, and that we often think about only when we wake up at three o'clock in the morning. The rest of the time when we are alone we have the radio or the television on—anything to avoid being alone with ourselves. Pascal maintained the sole reason for our unhappiness is that we are unable to sit alone in our room. He claimed we do not like to confront the reality of our lives; the human condition is so basically unhappy that we do everything to keep distracted from thinking about it. (*The Real Issue*, vol. 16, number 2, January 1997, 9)

Thus Thomas Jefferson addressed this question of worldview when he wrote to Henry Fry on June 17, 1804, of the "doctrines of Jesus" that contained the "sublimest system of morality,"

> I consider the doctrines of Jesus as delivered by himself to contain the outlines of the sublimest system of morality that has ever been taught but I hold in the most profound detestation and execration the corruptions of it which have been invented by priestcraft and established by kingcraft constituting a conspiracy of church and state against the civil and religious liberties of mankind.

Jefferson's point is that we must avoid the establishment of a state religion if we would preserve our civil and religious liberties, but we must also recognize that our culture needs a cohesive moral structure, and the best that Jefferson was aware of was the Judeo-Christian system. Our founders understood the clear difference between the life of the church and the essential presence of God in the sphere of the American conception of government.

George Washington also emphasized the cultural importance of the Judeo-Christian faith in his two great farewell messages. Leaving his role as Commanding General of the Revolutionary Army, he wrote to all thirteen state governors, emphasizing the cultural virtues of the Judeo-Christian system:

> I now make it my earnest prayer, that God would have you, and the State over which you preside, in his holy protection, that he would incline the hearts of the Citizens to cultivate a spirit of subordination and obedience to Government, to entertain a brotherly affection and love for one another, for their

fellow Citizens of the United States at large, and
particularly for their brethren who have served in
the Field, and finally, that he would most graciously
be pleased to dispose us all, to do Justice, to love
mercy, and to demean ourselves with that Charity,
humility and pacific temper of mind, which were
the Characteristicks of the Divine Author of our
blessed Religion, and without an humble imitation
of whose example in these things, we can never hope
to be a happy Nation.*

**(2) What you have termed a "watered down faith" is really an essential "worldview" which has a positive influence on the nation.**

So, while you are correct that "government" tends to water down true
religion, you must not mistake culture for the church. They are very different
and ought always be kept distinct. Simply put, the Gospel is not culture, but
the Gospel ought to leaven culture. An illustration that may be meaningful
here is the idea of "the home field advantage" in athletic competition. Simply
ask yourself, is it easier to carry out the work of the Gospel in the United States
or in Saudi Arabia or China? Why is that? The answer is the historic cultural
context in which that religious life is being exercised. I think this was part of
Paul's point when he wrote in 1 Timothy 2:1-3, "I urge, then, first of all, that
requests, prayers, intercession and thanksgiving be made for everyone—for
kings and all those in authority, that we may live peaceful and quiet lives in all
godliness and holiness. This is good, and pleases God our Savior..."

The impact of faith on a nation was recognized by William Bradford,
governor of Plymouth Plantation. In 1647, he wrote his classic work, *Of
Plymouth Plantation*. Therein he declares:

Thus out of small beginnings greater things have
been produced by His hand that made all things of
nothing, and gives being to all things that are; and as
one small candle may light a thousand, so the light
here kindled has shone to many, yea in some sort to
our whole nation; let the glorious name of Jehovah
have all the praise.

A classic example of faith as a positive influence on the whole nation in crisis is found in President Abraham Lincoln who, on March 30, 1863, when he called for a fast with these eloquent and moving words:

> Whereas, it is the duty of nations as well as of men to own their dependence upon the overruling power of God, to confess their sins and transgressions in humble sorrow yet with assured hope that genuine repentance will lead to mercy and pardon, and to recognize the sublime truth, announced in the Holy Scriptures and proven by all history: that those nations only are blessed whose God is the Lord:
>
> And, insomuch as we know that, by His divine law, nations like individuals are subjected to punishments and chastisement in this world, may we not justly fear that the awful calamity of civil war, which now desolates the land may be but a punishment inflicted upon us for our presumptuous sins to the needful end of our national reformation as a whole people?
>
> We have been the recipients of the choicest bounties of Heaven. We have been preserved these many years in peace and prosperity. We have grown in numbers, wealth and power as no other nation has ever grown.
>
> But we have forgotten God. We have forgotten the gracious Hand which preserved us in peace, and multiplied and enriched and strengthened us; and we have vainly imagined, in the deceitfulness of our hearts, that all these blessings were produced by some superior wisdom and virtue of our own.
>
> Intoxicated with unbroken success, we have become too self-sufficient to feel the necessity of redeeming and preserving grace, too proud to pray to the God that made us!

> It behooves us then to humble ourselves before
> the offended Power, to confess our national sins and
> to pray for clemency and forgiveness... All this
> being done, in sincerity and truth, let us then rest
> humbly in the hope authorized by the Divine
> teachings, that the united cry of the nation will be
> heard on high and answered with blessing no less
> than the pardon of our national sins and the
> restoration of our now divided and suffering country
> to its former happy condition of unity and peace.

Thus, the question is this: which worldview will provide the cultural "home field advantage" for the intersection of competing philosophies? Will it be, to name but a few competing philosophies: Christianity, Islam, secular humanism, scientism, post-modernity, radical homosexuality, or communism?[48]

### (3) Judeo-Christian Values Profoundly Impacted Culture in the Civil Rights Movement.

So while the state cannot present the "purity" of the Gospel as the church can and must, it can recognize, support, and encourage the historic values of the Judeo-Christian system which include justice, compassion, and community. In this context, I think we can learn a great deal from the wisdom of Dr. Martin Luther King, Jr. in his famous *Letter From Birmingham Jail*, written in April 1963.

Indeed, we must recognize that the state can corrupt the justice that God wants for His people by unjust laws, and the Church can choose to acquiesce in those laws. This came to a dramatic head in the issues of segregation and desegregation in the South in the last century. Many churches chose to take the position that removed the Church's life from the problems of culture. Consider the significant argument that Dr. King develops in his *Letter*:

> In the midst of a mighty struggle to rid our nation
> of racial and economic injustice, I have heard many
> ministers say: "Those are social issues, with which
> the gospel has no real concern." And I have watched

many churches commit themselves to a completely other worldly religion which makes a strange, unbiblical distinction between body and soul, between the sacred and the secular.... There was a time when the church was very powerful, in the time when the early Christians rejoiced at being deemed worthy to suffer for what they believed. In those days the church was not merely a thermometer that recorded the ideas and principles of popular opinion; it was a thermostat that transformed the mores of society. Whenever the early Christian entered a town, the people in power became disturbed and immediately sought to convict the Christians for being "disturbers of the peace" and "outside agitators." But the Christians pressed on, in the conviction that they were "a colony of heaven," called to obey God rather than man. Small in number, they were big in commitment. They were too God intoxicated to be "astronomically intimidated." By their effort and example they brought an end to such ancient evils as infanticide and gladiatorial contests.

Yet the church's indifference to social concern has damaged it. How different was the early church in its powerful testimony, as it rejoiced at being deemed worthy to suffer for her beliefs. The contemporary church is too often weak with an ineffectual voice.

Things are different now. So often the contemporary church is a weak, ineffectual voice with an uncertain sound. So often it is an arch defender of the status quo. Far from being disturbed by the presence of the church, the power structure of the average community is consoled by the church's silent and often even vocal sanction of things as they are.

Dr. King had no despair for the future, because he was convinced that God's will and America's sacred heritage was freedom.

*Dr. Martin Luther King – "the sacred heritage of our nation and the eternal will of God are embodied in our echoing demands."*

> We will reach the goal of freedom in Birmingham, and all over the nation, because the goal of America is freedom. Abused and scorned though we may be, our destiny is tied up with America's destiny. Before the pilgrims landed at Plymouth, we were here. Before the pen of Jefferson etched the majestic words of the Declaration of Independence across the pages of history, we were here. For more than two centuries our forebears labored in this country without wages; they made cotton king; they built the homes of their masters while suffering gross injustice and shameful humiliation–and yet out of a bottomless vitality they continued to thrive and develop. If the inexpressible cruelties of slavery could not stop us, the opposition we now face will surely fail. We will win our freedom because the sacred heritage of our nation and the eternal will of God are embodied in our echoing demands.

The nonviolent protestors in the just cause of desegregation displayed true heroism in the midst of provocation, and revealed one of the most sacred values in the Judeo-Christian heritage, and thereby reflected the values of America's founding fathers.

> One day the South will know that when these disinherited children of God sat down at lunch counters, they were in reality standing up for what is

best in the American dream and for the most sacred values in our Judeo-Christian heritage, thereby bringing our nation back to those great wells of democracy which were dug deep by the Founding Fathers in their formulation of the Constitution and the Declaration of Independence.

To summarize, I agree with you that we must avoid all "trampling" on minorities, whether in race or religion. Yet, we must also seek to avoid all "trampling" on the just expression of true pluralism. The minority must not be dealt with unjustly by the majority. The majority must not be dealt with unjustly by the minority. That is the quest for a true pluralism.

However, if justice is to mean anything, it cannot possibly mean that we recognize only our government for our values and must act as though we are atheists by never making reference to a just and righteous God in a public place, lest we offend someone. What it does mean is that there must be a government willingness to recognize an historical heritage of a nation, and yet not present it in a way that forces the minority into accepting that view for rights and a legitimate standing in our free society.

A true and just multi-cultural diversity must affirm free speech, religious liberty within the limits of just laws, and the inescapable reality of a predominate worldview. A case in point here is dealing with the presence of the Muslim faith in America in the aftermath of September 11th.

As America embarks on its war against terrorism, we are reminded that some religious viewpoints cannot be freely exercised—such as jihad, or declaring a holy war that urges the wanton destruction of those who do not accept fundamentalist Islamic beliefs. There are other religious perspectives that are entitled to religious liberty—such as the theology of Islam that teaches peace and extends religious liberty to others. Indeed, at the very core of America's response to terrorism, there is a simultaneous affirmation of religious liberty and an attempt to define its proper limits.

In addressing this issue, I think you will agree that our nation should affirm the Judeo-Christian virtue of love for one's neighbor and justice for one's enemy over the Islamic doctrine of the destruction of one's enemies through the jihad or holy war. Certainly this is what nationally honored Martin Luther King Jr. meant when he wrote,

The other force is one of bitterness and hatred, and it comes perilously close to advocating violence. It is expressed in the various black nationalist groups that are springing up across the nation, the largest and best-known being Elijah Muhammad's Muslim movement. Nourished by the Negro's frustration over the continued existence of racial discrimination, this movement is made up of people who have lost faith in America, who have absolutely repudiated Christianity, and who have concluded that the white man is an incorrigible "devil."

I have tried to stand between these two forces, saying that we need emulate neither the "do-nothingism" of the complacent nor the hatred and despair of the black nationalist, for there is the more excellent way of love and nonviolent protest. I am grateful to God that through the influence of the Negro church, the way of nonviolence became an integral part of our struggle.

Dr. King was surely correct when he declared that the world is in dire need of creative extremists in the Christian virtue of love.

But though I was initially disappointed at being categorized as an extremist, as I continued to think about the matter, I gradually gained a measure of satisfaction from the label.

Was not Jesus an extremist for love: "Love your enemies, bless them that curse you, do good to them that hate you, and pray for them which despitefully use you, and persecute you."

Was not Amos an extremist for justice: "Let justice roll down like waters and righteousness like an ever-flowing stream."

Was not Paul an extremist for the Christian gospel: "I bear in my body the marks of the Lord

Jesus."

Was not Martin Luther an extremist: "Here I stand; I cannot do otherwise, so help me God."

And John Bunyan: "I will stay in jail to the end of my days before I make a butchery of my conscience."

And Abraham Lincoln: "This nation cannot survive half slave and half free."

And Thomas Jefferson: "We hold these truths to be self-evident, that all men are created equal ..."

So the question is not whether we will be extremists, but what kind of extremists we will be. Will we be extremists for hate or for love? Will we be extremists for the preservation of injustice or for the extension of justice? In that dramatic scene on Calvary's hill three men were crucified. We must never forget that all three were crucified for the same crime—the crime of extremism. Two were extremists for immorality, and thus fell below their environment. The other, Jesus Christ, was an extremist for love, truth and goodness, and thereby rose above his environment. Perhaps the South, the nation, and the world are in dire need of creative extremists.*

There is something to be said for a government that at least sees benefit in the Judeo-Christian tradition, rather than views it with disdain or fear as a threat to the society's well being. Ask yourself this simple question: Where is it easier to start a church: Boston or Baghdad? Where is it easier to have an open air Christian worship service: In Saudi Arabia or South Carolina? Where is it easier to openly critique the government in a religious newspaper op-ed piece: Beijing or Birmingham? For us the *Letter from Birmingham Jail* is a fact of history. For the Chinese the letter from Beijing jail is a clandestine act taken at the risk of one's own life at this very moment in time.

If we are able then, to distinguish between Judeo-Christian values in culture and the Christian faith itself, we will see that the state certainly has, may, and should use the first, while it cannot make laws to embrace, advance, or proclaim the second. This is not a watering down of the Christian faith, but a benefiting from its wonderful implications for social justice and community. Rather than fearing its tendency to water down the Gospel, let us encourage it to preserve the "home-field advantage" encouraged by the Christian faith. This only underscores what Franklin said, about the "Necessity of a Publick Religion."

# chapter 8

# IS THE GOVERNMENT'S WORLDVIEW PERSPECTIVE UNIMPORTANT

## AND/OR UNNECESSARY IN THE CHRISTIAN MISSION?

"There are many avenues available to us Christians for promoting our worldview. We do not need to harness the government into doing it for us."

Let us begin by recognizing that Christianity does not need human government to accomplish its mission. If it did, there would not have been an apostolic church. Further, let us reiterate that Christians should be determined to make sure that the First Amendment is recognized for its constitutional meaning. We do not want to harness government to be an engine of Christian evangelism. It never has been such in American government, and it should never be. But at the same time, let us not forget that the fundamental values that have enabled our American experiment in government include many Christian ideas. Consider the place where our discussion began, namely, the Pledge of Allegiance.

> I pledge allegiance to the flag of the United States
> of America, and to the republic for which it stands,
> one Nation under God, indivisible, with liberty and
> justice for all.

Consider the following significant religious ideas affirmed in this statement, that do not need the potentially offending "under God." First, a republic is the idea of shared power of leaders with people. Those religions that insist on monarchy or despotism would not agree. When Benjamin Franklin left the Constitutional Convention one day, a woman asked him, "What kind of government have you given us?" He perceptively answered, "A republic, if you can keep it." Republican government is a form of government that various early founders of America saw as a by-product of Christian and biblical thinking. Thus, they also saw it as a fragile gift that could easily be lost.[49]

Second, many religious communities may consider the idea of "liberty" to be inconsistent with their revealed holy book that demands absolute conformity, rather than liberty. Further, who is to define justice? Justice in a communist state looks very different than justice in an Islamic state, and again in a state that has been influenced by Christian ideas of a just and righteous God who provided the model for justice.

Finally, do liberty and justice belong to all, or only to those in power? The point here is that government always expresses a "religious view," what we have designated above as a "worldview," concerning such key ideas of leadership, liberty, and justice. Finally, let us recognize that our founders understood that these great virtues of republican government were only possible based on the notion of Divinely given inalienable rights that mandated the separation or balance of powers, precisely because of man's political depravity.

So, as I address your final point, let me make an observation that I think is very revealing for my understanding of what is at issue. Throughout your letter, I have been struck with what I perceive to be a common pattern. You tend to make much of little and little of much. When you expressed your worries about the pledge and the Ten Commandments, the reality is that there has been no real harm done by their existence in public. But when they are forced by court decree to leave, we have experienced a very dangerous initiative of judicial fiat withdrawing the remembrance and enjoyment of historic rights from the people. The fact that you do not express the least concern about this suggests that you minimize what is a maximal issue. When you express concern about how these things are blending church and state and how they will cost the minority religious groups their liberty and perhaps their tax dollars, you once again major on minors and minimize what ought to be major. The proof here is that this is exactly what has compelled President Bush to sign his executive order—the government through its various arms has actively minimized the religious liberty of religion to an entire class. But your remarks have suggested that this state of affairs is entirely fine, lest the separation of church and state be confused, when all the while, the First Amendment does not even speak of such a separation. To be unconcerned about the burning issue of the federal government with regard to faith-based initiatives and to vociferously support a profound reinterpretation of the First Amendment by our High Court's interpolation of a nonexistent phrase into the Constitution reminds me of what Jesus spoke of in his famous metaphor—swallowing camels and choking on gnats. I think your concerns are exactly opposite of where they ought to be, given our nation's history, the crisis of our nation's current culture war, and the very important distinction that we must make between the church's mission and worldview and the role of a worldview in the broader culture.

As we conclude then, let us look briefly, at (1) The Minimizing of the Culture War Context of our Discussion About the Impact of the Christian Worldview on Government; (2) The Misunderstanding of the Church's Mission and How Church and Culture Ought to Relate; (3) Liberty Must Be Coupled with Moral Character for the Establishment and Continuation of a Free People in a Free Nation. (4) As Christians, We Are to be Salt and Light in All of Life, Including Culture and Politics.

## (1) The Minimizing of the Culture War Context of our Discussion About the Impact of the Christian Worldview on Government

Early patriot and martyr Nathan Hale's final words still produce awe, "I only regret that I have but one life to give for my country." The stirring words of Patrick Henry have lost none of their power over the centuries: "Is life so dear, and peace so sweet, as to be purchased at the price of chains and slavery? Forbid it, Almighty God! I know not what course others may take; but as for me, give me liberty or give me death!"*

*General Omar N. Bradley – "We have grasped the mystery of the atom and rejected the Sermon on the Mount."*

But what is the state of the soul of "the land of the free" at the start of the new millennium? At the end of World War II, as the cold war began, General Omar Bradley said, "We have grasped the mystery of the atom and rejected the Sermon on the Mount. . . .The world has achieved brilliance without conscience. Ours is a world of nuclear giants and ethical infants."* Thus America, now at the end of the cold war, is in the midst of yet another war—a culture war over the role of religion in public life. The salvos of our cultural battles powerfully impact family, government, school, church, media, and the individual.

All of us are aware of the deep tensions that divide the family and the government over which values are to be taught in the schools. "America has a population as religious as India's, presided over by an elite as secular as Sweden's," writes sociologist Peter Berger. In the many church-state battles over schools since the late 1940s, the secular elite has usually won, constantly expanding the once-narrow definition of what constitutes an establishment of religion. So, instead of government neutrality on religious questions, we have an atmosphere of aggressive, hostile secularity diminishing historical religious values in the schools. The late Supreme Court Justice Arthur Goldberg once called this attitude 'a brooding and pervasive devotion to the secular and a passive, or even active, hostility to religion.' For every religious American who wants the schools to push religion, a move that would be clearly unconstitutional, there are probably ten who have something much more modest in mind: protecting their children from an educational system that promotes values profoundly at odds with their religious convictions."[50]

Would Benjamin Franklin recognize America today considering that he taught, "A Bible and a newspaper in every house, a good school in every district—all studied and appreciated as they merit—are the principal support of virtue, morality, and civil liberty"?[51]

Conflict rages between church and state over the role of religious activity in the legislative arena. Paradoxically, even the church resists the state's occasional efforts to further spiritual values. Rev. Barry W. Lynn was quoted:

> Obviously, the House of Representatives is hopelessly adrift. Our nation faces serious problems, but all the House can offer are pious platitudes and meaningless resolutions ... Calling people to prayer and worship is the job of our houses of worship. If the House has nothing better to do than stomp all over religious turf, then it's time for them to take a summer vacation.

In this same article citing Rev. Lynn, the author writes,

> A non-binding resolution calling for a national day of prayer and fasting failed in the House yesterday [June 29], as Congress waded once again into volatile issues of religion and politics ... The bill also urged leaders in national, state and local governments — as well as in business —to call on the people they serve to observe "a day of solemn prayer. – Our nation is sick and hurting, and now is the time when all Americans of faith must come together and pray for healing and spiritual renewal,"(Rep. Helen Chenoweth, author of the

bill) said. If there ever is a time when we need almighty God, it is now.[52]

What would President John Adams think of Rev. Lynn's opposition to national prayer? Our second president said on March 6, 1799,

> As no truth is more clearly taught in the Volume of Inspiration, nor any more fully demonstrated by the experience of all ages, than that a deep sense and a due acknowledgment of the growing providence of a Supreme Being and of the accountableness of men to Him as searcher of hearts and righteous distributor of rewards and punishments are conducive equally to the happiness of individuals and to the well-being of communities. . . .I have thought proper to recommend, and I hereby recommend accordingly, that Thursday, the twenty-fifth day of April next, be observed throughout the United Sates of America as a day of solemn humiliation, fasting, and prayer.[53]

The poignant antithesis between liberalism and those who desire cultural spiritual renewal is described by Judge Robert H. Bork.

> The defining characteristics of modern liberalism are radical egalitarianism (the equality of outcomes rather than of opportunities) and radical individualism (The drastic reduction of limits to personal gratification). – Modern liberalism is powerful because it has enlisted our cultural elites, those who man the institutions that manufacture, manipulate, and disseminate ideas, attitudes, and symbols — universities, churches, Hollywood, the national press (print and electronic), foundation staffs, the "public interest" organizations, much of the congressional Democratic Party and some

congressional Republicans as well, and large sections of the judiciary, including, all to often, a majority of the Supreme Court. – One must never underestimate what Richard John Neuhaus called "the profound bigotry and anti-intellectualism and intolerance and illiberality of liberalism." – What may be feasible is a moral regeneration and intellectual understanding capable of defeating modern liberalism. In a discussion of that possibility with friends, we came up with four events that could produce a moral and spiritual regeneration: a religious revival; the revival of public discourse about morality; a cataclysmic war; or a deep economic depression. —Religion supplies the major premises from which moral reasoning begins.[54]

This liberal movement was already self-consciously at work in the late 1800's.[55]

Philip Schaff, a prominent church historian of the late eighteen hundreds, who taught at Union Theological Seminary in New York City, discussed this developing movement in *Church and State in the United States*. He quotes from the organ of the *Liberal League, The Index* (Jan. 4, 1873) as follows:

**The Demands Of Liberalism**

1.  We demand that churches and other ecclesiastical property shall no longer be exempted from just taxation.
2.  We demand that the employment of chaplains in Congress, in State Legislatures, in the navy and militia, and in prisons, asylums, and all other institutions supported by public money, shall be discontinued.
3.  We demand that all public appropriations for sectarian, educational, and charitable institutions shall cease.
4.  We demand that all religious services now sustained by the government shall be abolished; and especially that the use of the

Bible in the public schools, whether ostensibly as a text-book, or avowedly as a book of religious worship, shall be prohibited.

5. We demand that the appointment, by the President of the United States or by the Governors of the various states, of all religious festivals and feasts shall wholly cease.

6. We demand that the judicial oath in the courts, and in all other departments of the government, shall be abolished, and that simple affirmation under pains and penalties of perjury shall be established in its stead.

7. We demand that all laws, directly or indirectly, enforcing the observance of Sunday as the Sabbath shall be repealed.

8. We demand that all laws looking to the enforcement of "Christian" morality shall be abrogated, and that all laws shall be conformed to the requirements of natural morality, equal rights, and impartial liberty.

9. We demand that not only in the Constitutions of the United States and of the several States, but also in the practical administration of the same, no privilege or advantage shall be conceded to Christianity or any other special religion; that our entire political system shall be founded and administered on a purely secular basis; and that whatever changes shall prove necessary to this end shall be consistently, unflinchingly, and promptly made.

On the basis of this published agenda, Schaff accused the Liberal League of attempting "to heathenize the Constitution and to denationalize Christianity." Schaff then remarks:

> To carry out their program, the Free-thinkers would have to revolutionize public sentiment, to alter the constitutions and laws of the country, to undo or repudiate our whole history, to unchristianize the nation, and sink it below the heathen standard.

Marcellus Kik goes on to comment,

Little did he dream that a segment of his own denomination would seek to give reality to what he termed an "infidel program.*

President Theodore Roosevelt, however, recognized his place in one of America's "Christian institutions" when he said in 1909,

> After a week on perplexing problems. . .it does so rest my soul to come into the house of the Lord and to sing and mean it, "Holy, Holy, Holy, Lord God Almighty". . .(my) great joy and glory that, in occupying an exalted position in the nation, I am enabled, to preach the practical moralities of the Bible to my fellow-countrymen and to hold up Christ as the hope and Savior of the world.*

Roosevelt saw the looming potential for a radical cultural sea change when, in 1909 he also declared,

> Progress has brought us both unbounded opportunities and unbridled difficulties. Thus, the measure of our civilization will not be that we have done much, but what we have done with that much. I believe that the next half century will determine if we will advance the cause of Christian civilization or revert to the horrors of brutal paganism. The thought of modern industry in the hands of Christian charity is a dream worth dreaming. The thought of industry in the hands of paganism is a nightmare beyond imagining. The choice between the two is upon us.*

Roosevelt's half century brought America to 1959. In 1962-63, the Bible and prayer were banished from America's schools.[56] In 1973, abortion on demand was legalized as the indispensable corollary of the sexual revolution.[57] If America ever was a "Christian nation," after 1970, it certainly would be one no longer—American government must be secular, and religion must be exclusively a private matter.[58] In the 1980s, the Ten Commandments, along with other evidences of America's historical interest in Christianity, were stripped from the walls of public buildings.[59] In the early 1990s, our culture was inundated by the issues of gay-rights[60] and euthanasia.[61] Today, the legitimization of so-called "same-sex marriage" is being pursued throughout the courts of our land. Roosevelt's prescience is astonishing.[62]

Perhaps you are not aware of it, but the ways in which you have minimized the important and maximized the less threatening indicates the substantial extent to which your own thinking has been influenced by the agenda of "liberalism," as identified in their 1873 demands!

### (2) The Misunderstanding of the Church's Mission and How Church and Culture Ought to Relate

Another problem I perceive with your concern about connecting the Christian worldview with government is that it interpolates a mistaken view of how church and culture relate in our shared Judeo-Christian worldview. I believe the problem you fear actually reveals an unwarranted assumption that one can consistently hold both a Judeo-Christian worldview and yet have a view of the absolute neutrality of government and the admissibility of the government's imposing neutrality on its citizens with respect to their relationship to God and moral values. This view is, in fact, not Judeo-Christian, but actually an aspect of secular enlightenment thought in "sheep's clothing." By and large, except for some pacifistic forms of Christianity, our faith has always believed that Christian values have great implications for the conduct of good government—in terms of issues such as taxes, citizenship, justice, education, respect for authority, just war, limits of power, etc. Keep in mind the concept of the "home-field advantage" we discussed.

I, for one, am truly grateful that the Christian concept of religious liberty has been embraced by the world's most influential international governmental organization, The United Nations. The *UN Universal Declaration on Human Rights* declares:

> Everyone has the right to freedom of thought,
> conscience and religion; this right includes freedom
> to change his religion or belief, and freedom, either

alone or in community with others and in public or private, to manifest his religion or belief in teaching, practice, worship and observance.

US Supreme Court Justice David Josiah Brewer – "This republic is classified among the Christian nations of the world. It was so formally declared by the Supreme Court of the United States."

But isn't it interesting that it is only the nations with a Christian cultural heritage that actually live out this position that all United Nation participants have allegedly espoused?

That America was once a "Christian nation" actually has far more to do with its worldview and far less to do with its explicit constitutional statements. Consider here a fascinating, although clearly dated, statement from a legal scholar from America's past. In his work, *The United States — A Christian Nation*, Supreme Court Justice David Josiah Brewer wrote:

We classify nations in various ways. As, for instance, by their form of government. One is a kingdom, another an empire, and still another a republic. Also by race. Great Britain is an Anglo-Saxon nation, France a Gallic, Germany a Teutonic, Russia a Slav. And still again by religion. One is a Mohammedan nation, others are heathen, and still others are Christian nations. This republic is classified among the Christian nations of the World. It was so formally declared by the Supreme Court of the United States. But in what sense can it be called a Christian nation? Not in the sense that Christianity is the established religion or that the people are in any manner compelled to support it. On the contrary, the Constitution specifically provides that "Congress shall make no law respecting an establishment of religion, or prohibiting the free exercise thereof." Neither is it Christian in the sense that a profession of Christianity is a condition of holding office or otherwise engaging in the public service, or essential to recognition either politically or socially. In fact the government as a legal organization is independent of all religions. Nevertheless, we constantly speak of this republic as a Christian nation—in fact, as the leading Christian nation of the world. This popular use of the term certainly has significance. It is not a mere creation of the imagination. It is not a term of derision, but has a substantial basis—one which justifies its use.[63]

Scholar Marcelus Kik, helpfully explains the idea of the impact of the Judeo-Christian worldview on a State.

Western civilization owes much in its laws and institutions to Christian inspiration. The influence of Christian principles has been a definite blessing to the United States and the attempt to remove all traces of Christianity from public institutions shows abysmal ignorance of the source of America's greatness and stability. A State whose laws and institutions are influenced by Christian life and principles is a blessing both for true religion and for civil liberty…

To isolate God from government is worse than heathenism, for heathenism at least acknowledges the existence of some form of deity. Governments have a responsibility to God, inasmuch as they have been ordained by Him, and their actions therefore take on a moral character. Those who framed the federal Constitution recognized this fact and so erected a legal wall between Church and State—but not a moral and spiritual bulwark, nor one that separated either one or both parties from God and His laws.*

*The Constitution of the United States*

**(3) Liberty Must Be Coupled with Moral Character for the Establishment and Continuation of a Free People in a Free Nation.**

Perhaps you remember the poignant words of Madame Roland, a heroine of the French Revolution and lover of liberty who cried as she was led to the guillotine, "O Liberty! How many crimes are committed in thy name!" Her words here underscore what I'm trying to say, namely, there is a "worldview necessity" for morality and religious concerns in our government. This is not to ask the state to do the "mission" work of the church. It is not to harness the government to teach the church's values. Rather, it is to recognize the truth of what our founders expressed: Our American form of government depends for its existence and health on values that emerge from the Judeo-Christian worldview.

Several historical examples underscore this "worldview necessity" of Judeo-Christian virtues and for effective American government.

- The preamble of the Constitution highlights the quest for and value of several Judeo-Christian virtues: union, justice, peace, general welfare, blessings of liberty, and multi-generationism.

> We the People of the United States, in Order to form a more perfect Union, establish Justice, insure domestic Tranquility, provide for the common defence, promote the general Welfare, and secure the Blessings of Liberty to ourselves and our Posterity, do ordain and establish this Constitution for the United States of America.

- Early founder William Penn said in his Preface to the Frame of Government,

> Liberty without obedience is confusion and obedience without liberty is slavery....governments, like clocks, go from the motion men give them, as governments are made and moved by men, so by them they are ruined too. Wherefore governments rather depend upon men, than men upon governments. Let men do good, and the

government cannot be bad; if it be ill, they will cure it. But if men be bad, let the government be never so good, they will endeavor to warp and spoil it to their turn. I know some say, let us have good laws, and no matter for the men that execute them: but let them consider, that though good laws do well, good men do better: for good laws may want [i.e. lack] good men, and be abolished or invaded by ill men; but good men will never want [i.e. lack] good laws, nor suffer ill ones… That therefore, which makes a good constitution, must keep it, viz: men of wisdom and virtue, qualities, that because they descend not with worldly inheritances, must be carefully propagated by a virtuous education of youth... (William Penn, *Preface, Frame of Government 1683)*

• James Madison, for example, declared at the Virginia Convention on June 20, 1788, underscoring a view that we saw above in George Washington:

To suppose that any form of government will secure liberty or happiness without any virtue in the people, is a chimerical idea.

• Our second president, John Adams underscored this belief in his address to the military, dated October 11, 1798:

We have no government armed with power capable of contending with human passions unbridled by morality and religion. Avarice, ambition, revenge, or gallantry, would break the strongest cords of our Constitution as a whale goes through a net. Our Constitution was made only for a moral and religious people. It is wholly inadequate to the government of any other.

• Similarly on August 28, 1811, Adams wrote:

> Religion and virtue are the only foundations, not
> only of republicanism and of all free government,
> but of social felicity under all governments and in
> all the combinations of human society.

• Moreover, this early view was carried forward by our later presidents as well. President Harry S. Truman affirmed:

> The fundamental basis of this nation's laws was
> given to Moses on the Mount. The fundamental
> basis of our Bill of Rights comes from the teachings
> we get from Exodus and St. Matthew, from Isaiah
> and St. Paul. I don't think we emphasize that
> enough these days. If we don't have a proper
> fundamental moral background, we will finally end
> up with a totalitarian government which does not
> believe in rights for anybody except the State!*

• Dwight D. Eisenhower said in 1957:

> The blessing of life and the freedoms all of us enjoy
> in this land today are based in no small measure on
> the Ten Commandments, which have been handed
> down to us by the religious teachers of the Jewish
> faith. These Commandments of God provide
> endless opportunities for fruitful service, and they
> are a stronghold of moral purpose for men
> everywhere.*

While you may firmly believe that the government's supporting worldview is not needed for the church to do its work, let us remember that it is surely easier for the church to do its work from outside the catacombs than from within them. Moreover, as I look at the eroding force of faith in the public square, and the creeping hostility of the secularist worldview vis-à-vis the

Christian worldview, there seems to me to be fewer and fewer avenues of promotion of the Christian faith in our culture.

Because of this constant advance of secularist hostility to the Christian worldview, there is often an unthinking unconscious acquiescence of all too many Christians to its faith-tenet of the alleged "neutrality" of government. While the ancient church taught us all well that we do not need the government's support of our worldview to advance our faith, the ancient church taught this truth alongside of Tertullian's costly lesson: "The blood of the martyrs is the seed of the Church."*

So then, I do not desire the state to carry out the church's mission. However, I do not wish to give up a friendly home-field playing advantage without a fight. For if we continue to lose ground as to where the Christian worldview is deemed acceptable by the prevailing cultural zeitgeist, it will not just be the government and the schools and the public square where the church will be silenced by governmental force, but it will also soon be in the church and in the home as well. Given that somber reality, I intend to stay engaged in the culture war in the public square before the forces of the state enter even further into either my pulpit or my living room.

### (4) As Christians, We are to be Salt and Light in All of Life, Including Culture and Politics.

We must rediscover the Christian's role of being what Jesus described as "salt and light" in Matthew 5:13-16. Salt preserves and purifies. Light dispels darkness. When we live out our Christian values we preserve and purify our culture. We begin to dispel the darkness of injustice and ungodliness. Some have described the task of being salt and light as fulfilling the "cultural mandate." The idea of the "cultural mandate" emerges from Genesis 1:28, where we find the words, "God blessed them and said, 'Be fruitful and increase...fill the earth, and subdue it. Rule over the fish of the sea and the birds of the air and over every living creature that moves on the ground.'" Dr. James Kennedy writes:

> What is the Cultural Mandate? We are to take all
> the potentialities of this world, all of its spheres and
> institutions, and bring them all to the glory of God.
> We are to use this world to the glory of God. We

are to bring it and surrender it at the foot of the Cross. In every aspect of the world, we are to bring glory to God and this means in all of the institutions of the world. (D. James Kennedy, *What If Jesus Had Never Been Born?*, [Thomas Nelson, 1994], 240)

Many years ago, J. Gresham Machen explained the importance of impacting one's culture for the sake of effectively communicating the Christian Gospel,

It would be a great mistake to suppose that all men are equally well prepared to receive the Gospel. But God usually exerts that power in connection with certain prior conditions of the human mind, and it should be ours to create, so far as we can, with the help of God, those favorable conditions for the reception of the Gospel. False ideas are the greatest obstacle to the reception of the Gospel. We may preach with all the fervor of a reformer and yet succeed only in winning a straggler here and there, if we permit the whole collective thought of the nation to be controlled by ideas which prevent Christianity from being regarded as anything more than a harmless delusion. (J. Gresham Machen, "Christianity & Culture" *The Princeton Theological Review*, Vol. II, 1913, 7)[64]

*J. Gresham Machen – "False ideas are the greatest obstacle to the reception of the Gospel."*

As George Grant writes, cultural engagement or political involvement can never be an end in itself for a Christian:

Christians should never become involved in political action if this is the limit of our vision. If our sights are set simply on enhancing or influencing or aggrandizing the present world system, then we should forget it altogether... True Christian cultural involvement action seeks to rein the passions of men and curb the pattern of digression under God's rule. (*Changing of the Guard*, [Broadman and Holman, 1995], 82)

But because the Christian has the truth of God, his calling is to impact all of life with his spiritual life. Francis Schaeffer put it this way,

True spirituality covers all of reality. There are things the Bible tells us as absolutes which are sinful—which do not conform to the character of God. But aside from these the Lordship of Christ covers all of life equally...Christianity is not just a series of truths but Truth—Truth about all of reality. And the holding to that Truth intellectually brings forth not only certain personal results, but also governmental and legal results. (Francis Schaeffer, *A Christian Manifesto*, [Crossway Books, 1981], 20)

*Francis Schaeffer-"Christianity is not just a series of truths but Truth—Truth about all of reality."*

The point of all of this is to emphasize that someone's worldview will control the public square. If we as Christians are not involved in the life of our culture, the Christian worldview will be unheard and will be the kind of salt that will only be trampled underfoot of men, since it has lost its saltiness.

# chapter 9

# GEORGE WASHINGTON'S CONSTITUTIONAL PRECEDENTS FOR

## THE CENTRALITY OF THE JUDEO-CHRISTIAN VALUES IN THE PUBLIC SQUARE.

"There are many avenues available to us Christians for promoting our worldview. We do not need to harness the government into doing it for us."

*George Washington – "We may then unite in most humbly offering our prayers and supplications to the great Lord and Ruler of Nations."*

Your comment also raises the question of whether our founding fathers, and specifically, our first president, George Washington, saw a legitimate relationship between government and the Christian worldview.

Everyone agrees that George Washington was critical for the formation of America's values. Washington was conscious that his every act created a precedent for good or ill for all that would follow him.[65] As our first president, everything he did established precedents for how our country was to work.

So there is no accident that so many have sought to portray Washington as a man without faith. For if he exercised faith in the public square, this in turn argues that the Judeo-Christian system still has relevance and vitality in the public square today. Did Washington's legacy include strong precedents of advocating the Judeo-Christian values in the public square? Recent authors have declared an emphatic no. Randall writes, "Washington was not a deeply religious man."[66] Douglas Southall Freeman says, "He had believed that a God directed his path, but he had not been particularly ardent in his faith."[67] James Thomas Flexner states that "Washington …avoided, as was his deist custom, the word 'God.' "[68] Judging from these writers, Washington could hardly be called a "godly leader." But are these claims correct?

## (1) National Thanksgiving to Celebrate the Constitution

In recent decades, the First Amendment to the Constitution has been construed to mean that there must be a strict separation of church and state and that there should be no religious expression allowed in the public arena. The first sentence of the amendment simply says, "Congress shall make no law respecting an establishment of religion, nor prohibiting the free exercise thereof." The very men who gave us the First Amendment did not intend to impose a radical separation of church and state that is advocated by so many today. In fact, the day after Congress adopted the words of the First Amendment, they sent a message to President Washington, asking him to declare a day of thanksgiving to show America's appreciation to God for the opportunity to create America's new national government in peace and tranquility. So on October 3, 1789, President Washington made a Proclamation of a National Day of Thanksgiving. He declared:

> Whereas it is the duty of all nations to acknowledge the Providence of Almighty God, to obey His will, to be grateful for his benefits, and humbly to implore His protection and favor; and
>
> Whereas both Houses of Congress have by their joint Committee requested me "to recommend to the People of the United States a day of public thanksgiving and prayer to be observed by acknowledging with grateful hearts the many signal favors of Almighty God, especially by affording them an opportunity peaceably to establish a form of government for their safety and happiness;" Now, therefore, I do recommend and assign Thursday, the twenty-sixth day of November next, to be devoted by the People of these United States to the service of that great and glorious Being, who is the beneficent Author of all the good that was, that is, or that will be;
>
> That we may then all unite in rendering unto Him our sincere and humble thanks, for His kind care and protection of the People of this country previous to their becoming a Nation; for the signal and manifold mercies, and the favorable interpositions of His Providence, which we experienced in the course and conclusion of the late war; for the great degree of tranquillity, union, and plenty, which we have since enjoyed, for the peaceable and rational manner in which we have been enabled to establish constitutions of government for our safety and happiness, and particularly the national one now lately instituted,

for the civil and religious liberty with which we are blessed, and the means we have of acquiring and diffusing useful knowledge; and in general for all the great and various favors which He hath been pleased to confer upon us.

And also that we may then unite in most humbly offering our prayers and supplications to the great Lord and Ruler of Nations, and beseech Him to pardon our national and other transgressions, to enable us all, whether in public or private stations, to perform our several and relative duties properly and punctually; to render our national government a blessing to all the People, by constantly being a government of wise, just and constitutional laws, discreetly and faithfully executed and obeyed; to protect and guide all Sovereigns and Nations (especially such as have shown kindness unto us) and to bless them with good government, peace, and concord; to promote the knowledge and practice of true religion and virtue, and the increase of science among them and Us; and generally to grant unto all Mankind such a degree of temporal prosperity as He alone knows to be best.

Given under my hand, at the city of New York, the 3rd of October, in the year of our Lord one thousand seven hundred and eighty-nine.[69]

One cannot read those words without realizing how the founders and "father of our nation" did *not* intend for God to be separated from our official acts. Rather, the founders just did not want a national denomination, as they had experienced in England. They did not want to have an established church, since an established church took away religious liberty. So, the federal government was carefully designed to assure that there would not be an official state church that could force people to worship against their will, or could coerce people to support with their tax dollars.

## (2) The Constitution: Human Depravity Requires Limited Power

Washington had learned by brutal experience the difficulties the Continental Congress had in getting the necessary work done to care for the army. Toward the end of the war, as we observed in the last chapter, he began to call for plans to strengthen the powers of government for the good of the whole nation. Ultimately, his concerns were shared by many, and the Constitutional Convention was held in Philadelphia in 1789. Washington's religion manifested itself in various ways during that critical summer in Independence Hall.

Washington's years of experience with people in the business context taught him the importance of contracts, in light of human nature and what he termed "the rascality of Mankind." Writing to Lund Washington, he said,

> If this should be the case, it will be only adding to the many proofs we dayly see of the folly of leaving bargains unbound by solemn covenants. I see so many instances of the rascallity of Mankind, that I am almost out of conceit of my own species; and am convinced that the only way to make men honest, is to prevent their being otherwise, by tying them firmly to the accomplishmt. of their contracts.[70]

*Independence Hall, Philadelphia, in the 1700's*

The nation, too, needed a solemn covenant to assure its success. Washington's interest in a constitutional document is seen in the sheer frequency with which he speaks of the idea of the constitution. The word appears over four hundred times in his writings. Even at the start of the war in 1776, he understood the importance of preparing a sound constitution for excellent governance. Writing to his brother to encourage him in the Virginian effort to compose a new constitution,

Washington said.

> "Dear Brother: Since my arrival at this place, where
> I came at the request of Congress, to settle some
> matters relative to the ensuing Campaign I have
> received your Letter…To form a new Government,
> requires infinite care, and unbounded attention; for
> if the foundation is badly laid[,] the superstructure
> must be bad, too. Much time therefore, cannot be
> bestowed in weighing and digesting matters well.
> We have, no doubt, some good parts in our present
> constitution; many bad ones we know we have,
> wherefore no time can be misspent that is imployed
> in seperating the Wheat from the Tares. My fear is,
> that you will all get tired and homesick, the
> consequence of which will be, that you will patch up
> some kind of Constitution as defective as the
> present; this should be avoided, every Man should
> consider, that he is lending his aid to frame a
> Constitution which is to render Million's happy, or
> Miserable, and that a matter of such moment cannot
> be the Work of a day.[71]

When the U.S. Constitution was under consideration by the nation,
Washington himself became a keen political scientist in his own right. In fact,
he claimed to have read every available publication that appeared in the debate!
He wrote:

> The mind is so formed in different persons as to
> contemplate the same object in different points of
> view. Hence originates the difference on questions of
> the greatest import, both human and divine. In all
> Institutions of the former kind, great allowances are
> doubtless to be made for the fallibility and
> imperfection of their authors. Although the agency
> I had informing this system, and the high opinion I

entertained of my Colleagues for their ability and integrity may have tended to warp my judgment in its favour; yet I will not pretend to say that it appears absolutely perfect to me, or that there may not be many faults which have escaped my discernment. I will only say, that, during and since the Session of the Convention, I have attentively heard and read every oral and printed information of both sides of the question that could readily be procured. This long and laborious investigation, in which I endeavoured as far as the frailty of nature would permit to act with candour has resulted in a fixed belief that this Constitution, is really in its formation a government of the people; that is to say, a government in which all power is derived from, and at stated periods reverts to them, and that, in its operation, it is purely, a government of Laws made and executed by the fair substitutes of the people alone.[72]

From his unique vantage point of having presided at the Constitutional Convention, and from his expertise in pursuing the entirety of the debate, Washington addressed the question of the merits of the proposed Constitution. Simply put, he recognized that it was not perfect. The people who would be governed by it would not be perfect either, given human nature.

Writing to Lafayette on February 7, 1788, he expressed his view that the states' agreement on the Constitution was near miraculous. But he also admitted that there were defects in the document. But, his constitutional "creed" had "two great points": the Constitution gave no more power than necessary to have a good government, and there were constitutional checks and balances on the government's use

*The Marquis de Lafayette*

of power through popular rule and by the separation of powers among three branches that kept an eye on one another for the good of the nation.[73] Beyond this, the Constitution also provided for its own amendment, when citizens would find this necessary.[74]

Washington's religion manifested itself precisely at this point in the constitutional debate. The ideas he expressed by terms such as "limited power," "the separation of powers," "the rule of the people," "checks and balances," and the "need for amendment," all existed for one simple reason—people abuse power. The idea of the abuse of power and political depravity were openly admitted at the Constitutional Convention,[75] and also seriously pondered by Washington.[76] Political depravity is a theological concept that flows from the doctrine of human sinfulness—a basic postulate of Christian teaching. In fact, Washington asserted that human depravity could ultimately destroy the Constitution, even with the checks and balances it possessed. In his proposed Address to Congress in April 1789, he described how the Constitution, with all of its wisdom, could ultimately come to naught by the depravity of the people and those who govern them, since the Constitution in the hands of a corrupt people was a mere "wall of words" or a "mound of parchment."[77]

### (3) The Constitution and the "Completion of Our Happiness"

But if religion was present theologically in the Constitution, why was it not present explicitly or openly? This question was directly asked of Washington by the Presbyterian ministers and elders from the First Presbytery of the Eastward that included clergy from Massachusetts and New Hampshire. The New Englanders had a Christian commitment that was expressed through their established religion of the Congregational Church and the closely related Presbyterian tradition.[78] They had wished for a direct reference to the Christian faith in the Constitution, but their disappointment was entirely removed by the public and private Christian and pious leadership of Washington! They wrote:

> Whatever any may have supposed wanting in the original plan, we are happy to find so wisely providing in it amendments; and it is with peculiar satisfaction we behold how easily the entire confidence of the People, in the Man who sits at the

helm of Government, has eradicated every remaining objection to its form.

Among these we never considered the want of *a religious test*, that grand engine of persecution in every tyrant's hand: but we should not have been alone in rejoicing to have seen some Explicit acknowledgement of the *only true God and Jesus Christ, whom he hath sent* inserted some where in the *Magna Charta* of our country.

We are happy to find, however, that this defect has been amply remedied, in the face of all the world, by the piety and devotion, in which your first public act of office was performed—by the religious observance of the Sabbath, and of the public worship of *God*, of which you have set so eminent an example—and by the warm strains of Christian and devout affections, which run through your late proclamation, for a general thanksgiving.

The catholic spirit breathed in all your public acts supports us in the pleasing assurance that no religious establishments—no exclusive privileges tending to elevate one denomination of Christians to the depression of the rest shall ever be ratified by the signature of the *President* during your administration.

On the contrary we bless God that your whole deportment bids all denominations confidently to expect to find in you the watchful guardian of their equal liberties—the steady patron of genuine Christianity—and the bright Exemplar of those peculiar virtues, in which its distinguishing doctrines have their proper effect.

Under the nurturing hand of a Ruler of such virtues, and one so deservedly revered by all ranks, we joyfully indulge the hope that virtue and religion will revive and flourish—that infidelity and the vices ever attendant in its train, will be banished [from] every polite circle; and that rational piety will soon become fashionable there; and from thence be diffused among all other ranks in the community.[79]

These Presbyterians had not the least suspicion of any presidential deism. Did a deistic President Washington desire to correct their mistaken identification of him as the "bright Exemplar" and "steady patron of genuine Christianity"? Here truly was an occasion for a man of candor, honesty, character, honor, and truth to practice his maxim of "honesty is the best policy." Washington's candid reply did not sidestep the issue of the absence of a direct reference to Christianity in the Constitution. Nor did he miss the fact that his clerical correspondents had identified him as a great defender of Christianity, whose piety and actions had successfully assuaged their fears about the omission of such a reference to Christianity and the negative impact it might have had on the ongoing role of Christian faith under the Constitution. Washington's answer was actually theologically astute, as it is a direct allusion to a foundational Presbyterian doctrine—the perspicuity, clarity, or plainness of the Gospel in the scriptures:[80] The president wrote,

I am persuaded, you will permit me to observe that the path of true piety is so plain as to require but little political direction. To this consideration we ought to ascribe the absence of any regulation, respecting religion, from the Magna-Charta of our country. To the guidance of the ministers of the gospel[,] this important object is, perhaps, more properly committed. It will be your care to instruct the ignorant, and to reclaim the devious, and, in the progress of morality and science, to which our government will give every furtherance, we may confidently expect the advancement of true religion, and the completion of our happiness.[81]

In sum, Washington believed the Gospel was plain and did not need the Constitution to direct it, and this is why there is no explicit regulation concerning religion in the "Magna-Charta" of America. "Ministers of the gospel," such as the Presbyterian clergy whom he was addressing, were more appropriately given this evangelistic task. Yet Washington pledged his best efforts to further morality and science, which he was confident would result in the advancement not just of religion in general, but of "true religion."[82]

In context, this had direct reference to the Presbyterian clergy's phrase, the "Explicit acknowledgement of the *only true God and Jesus Christ, whom he hath sent.*" And as to the clergy's identification of Washington with the Christian faith, we find that he embraced this as well, for the expected advancement of true religion would not only result in the "completion" of the clergy's "happiness," a universally understood synonym for salvation in the era,[83] but in the completion of "our" happiness, inclusive of Washington himself.[84] The historical circumstances, the contextual frame of reference for Washington's letter, and his grammar make only one conclusion possible—Washington wanted the clergy to know that they were correct in identifying him as a Christian.

Here, then, we can see why Washington insisted that religion and morality were "indispensable pillars" of America's political happiness. We will consider the implications of this statement from his Farewell Address in the final section of this chapter.

## (4) A Presidential Sermon: Washington's First Inaugural Address

The man who refused to be king at the end of the war was unanimously chosen as president at the start of the new constitutional government—the only man to occupy that office who could make that claim. At his inauguration to the presidency, even as at his retirement from the military, he gave evidence for his Christian faith.

In his first Inaugural Address, Washington frequently referred to the Almighty. His very first act as president was to pray. Washington prayed that God would secure the liberties of the new nation:[85] He went on to say that no one should be more grateful to God than the people of the United States of America in light of what he (God) had done for them throughout the war.[86]

Although the new nation had just gone through the tumultuous time after the Revolution of creating a new civil government, this process fraught with sectional rivalries and tensions was accomplished in a peacefully unique way that called for "pious gratitude," since this implied even more divine blessings to come.[87] The implication Washington drew from all of this was that America could not expect the continuing "smiles of Heaven" if "the eternal rules of order and right which Heaven itself has ordained" were disregarded.[88]

We must remember that when Washington attended the Anglican churches of his day, he—along with the congregation—recited the Ten Commandments from the reredos behind the altar. In Washington's historical context, "the eternal rules of order and right which Heaven itself has ordained" could only refer to the Ten Commandments, given that this was the belief of almost every American in Washington's day who read or heard his Inaugural Address.

Along with his solemn Inaugural Address that graced America's first auspicious pageant of civil religion, Washington's inauguration contributed other religious precedents. He was sworn in as president with the use of the Bible. This Bible has been sacredly kept by the masons of New York City. The page where Washington placed his hand for the oath of office was marked by the turning down of the corner of the page. Interestingly, the marked page is Genesis 49, the chapter where Jacob, the father of the sons of Israel, bestows his blessing upon them. By this time Washington had long been called "the father of his country." The parallel of the text and the inauguration was not accidental. Tradition adds that he said, "So help me God!" as he took his oath, and then bent down and kissed the sacred book.[89]

But the religious elements of Washington's inauguration were still not complete. Next, he led the congressmen and everyone else across the street from Federal Hall to St. Paul's Chapel for a two-hour service of Christian worship to commit the new nation to God.[90] According to Mrs. Alexander Hamilton, she knelt with President Washington as they received the Eucharist together.[91]

### (5) Washington's Public Witness to the Religious Bodies of America

At various times during Washington's presidency, he had remarkable opportunities to declare his faith, as he was honored by various religious groups. These religious denominations often wrote an address to express their joy in Washington's actions, presence, words, or election to office. With remarkable consistency, Washington acknowledged these letters. In doing so, he also revealed in various ways his personal religious views. There are approximately thirty some addresses that Washington received from religious bodies and that he answered during his presidential years. They reflect the full spectrum of America's religious communities in his era, from both ecumenical clergy groups[92] and individual denominations, such as Roman Catholic,[93] Episcopal,[94] Lutheran,[95] German Reformed,[96] Dutch Reformed,[97] Presbyterian,[98] Congregational,[99] Moravian,[100] Methodist,[101] Baptist,[102] Quaker,[103] Masonic,[104] Universalist,[105] Jewish,[106] and Swedenborgian.[107] In all of his letters, Washington was always polite and clear.

Interestingly, there is no record of any deistic group or atheist group that wrote to Washington. We cannot fully summarize these letters here, but a careful reading of them will demonstrate that they consistently refer to God or divine Providence. They often quote or appeal to scripture, and consistently reflect a Christian faith and understanding on the part of Washington. They also consistently call for civil obedience and the maintenance of religious liberty. They often conclude with the need to pray for the nation or one another, with a wish of blessing for this life and the life hereafter.

These letters are some of the best commentaries on Washington's personal religion as well as his vision for the friendly and cooperative relationship between the distinct spheres of church and state. Most significantly for our purposes, not one of them provides a hint of a deistic unbelief on the part of Washington.

The characteristic spirit of this correspondence is that both Washington and his religious correspondents agreed that both sides represented godly and religious people. To demonstrate this, we will consider a few of the more salient examples. The Lutherans wrote on April 27, 1789, to the new President: "Pleasingly do we anticipate the blessings of a wise and efficient government—equal freedom—perfect safety—a sweet contentment spreading through the whole land—irreproachable manners with pure religion, and *that* righteousness which exalteth a Nation." In a most non-deistic manner, Washington responded, "I flatter myself opportunities will not be wanting for me to shew my disposition to encourage the domestic and public virtues of industry, economy, patriotism, philanthropy, and that righteousness which exalteth a nation. . . and amidst all the vicissitudes that may await me in this mutable state of existence, I shall earnestly desire the continuation of an interest in your intercessions at the Throne of Grace."[108]

The Methodist bishops had written to the president, ". . .we enjoy a holy expectation that you always will prove a faithful and impartial Patron of genuine, vital religion—the grand end of our creation and present probationary existence. And we promise you our fervent prayers to the Throne of Grace that GOD almighty may endue you with all the graces and gifts of his holy spirit, that may enable you to fill up your important station to his glory, the good of his Church, the happiness and prosperity of the United States, and the welfare of mankind."*

Washington's response could not have been that of a deist, unless it was the kind of deist that delighted in deceiving others by playing the role of a religious charlatan. Only a godly man could have sincerely written Washington's words to the Bishops: "After mentioning that I trust the people of every denomination, who demean themselves as good citizens, you will have occasion to be convinced that I shall always strive to prove a faithful and impartial Patron of genuine, vital religion; I must assure you in particular that I take in the kindest part the promise you make of presenting your prayers at the Throne of Grace for me, and that I likewise implore the divine benedictions on yourselves and your religious community."[109]

His opening line to the German Reformed Congregations on June 1789 was a simple and clear affirmation of Washington's perspective of his own personal piety, "I am happy in concurring with you in the sentiments of gratitude and piety towards Almighty-God, which are expressed with such fervency of devotion in your address; and in believing, that I shall always find in you, and the German Reformed Congregations in the United States a conduct correspondent to such worthy and pious expressions."[110] This does not sound like someone who "was not a deeply religious man," or someone who "had not been particularly ardent in his faith," or one who "avoided, as was his Deist custom, the word 'God.'"[111]

## (6) Presbyterian Praise for Presidential Piety

But Washington's seeming personal godliness not only touched the Lutherans and the Methodists, but the Presbyterians also saw in the president a deeply pious life of Christian faithfulness. The Moderator of the Presbyterian General Assembly, Rev. John Rodgers, who had corresponded with Washington during the war about giving Bibles to the American troops,[112] was a key signatory of a letter emanating from a committee of the General Assembly. The Presbyterians wrote,

We adore Almighty GOD the author of every perfect gift who hath endued you with such a rare and happy assemblage of Talents as hath rendered you equally necessary to your country in war and in peace . . . .the influence of your personal character moderates the divisions of political parties. . . .your present elevated station by the voice of a great and free people, and with an unanimity of suffrage that has few if any examples in history…their confidence in your virtues; . . . we derive a presage even more flattering from the piety of your character. . . .a steady, uniform, avowed friend of the Christian religion, who has commenced his administration in rational and exalted sentiments of Piety, and who in his private conduct adorns the doctrines of the Gospel of Christ, and on the most public and solemn occasions devoutly acknowledges the government of divine Providence. The examples of distinguished Characters will ever possess a powerful and extensive influence on the public mind, and when we see in such a conspicuous station the amiable example of piety to God, of benevolence to men, and of a pure and virtuous patriotism, we naturally hope that it will diffuse its influence and that eventually the most happy consequences will result from it.[113]

Was the Presbyterian committee utterly mistaken about the godliness they had observed in Washington? Their letter bristled with affirmations of Washington's piety—"personal character," "virtues," "piety of your character," "avowed friend of the Christian religion," "rational and exalted sense of piety," "his private conduct adorns the doctrines of the Gospel of Christ," "devoutly acknowledges the government of divine Providence," "amiable example of piety to God," "a pure and virtuous patriotism."

Washington's response to this litany of Presbyterian praise for his spiritual devotion revealed the temperament of a sincere Christian, not the temporizing of a mere politician. First and last, his concern for humility shone through: "…it will be my endeavor to avoid being elated by the too favorable opinion which your kindness for me may have induced you to express….I desire you to accept my acknowledgements for your…prayers to Almighty God for his blessing on our common country and the humble instrument, which he has been pleased to make use of in the administration of its government."[114]

But Washington also understood the essence of the Presbyterian letter. They were declaring their belief that Washington himself was a Christian. What was Washington's response to this? Was it an evasion that would allow for his actual deism to stand without causing offense to his religious well-wishers?

Instead, his answer was one that reflected a deep sense of faith and dependence upon God: "I reiterate the possession of my dependence upon Heaven as the source of all public and private blessings." His answer also reflected the importance of the kind of piety the Presbyterians had just extolled in him: "I will observe that the general prevalence of piety, philanthropy, honesty, industry and economy seems, in the ordinary course of human affairs are particularly necessary for advancing and confirming the happiness of our country."

Finally, his answer emphasized that authentic Christianity was a matter to be prized, pursued and proven. While Washington's classic vocabulary might cloud our understanding, we can sense the passion for the Christian faith that motivated his words. His central thought was this, since all Americans enjoyed full religious liberty, it was only reasonable that something would be expected from them in return for this great blessing.[115] What was this? Washington said, "…that they will be emulous of evincing the sincerity of their profession by the innocence of their lives, and the beneficence of their actions."

We need some help here to understand Washington's intent. A modern equivalent of Washington's staid and archaic eighteenth-century rhetoric is: "they [i.e., religious Americans] will be ambitious to surpass others in demonstrating convincingly their heartfelt declaration of faith by the sinlessness of their lives and the kindness of their actions." Why must one's faith be demonstrated by such works? Washington's answer stated: "For no man, who is profligate in his morals, or a bad member of the civil community, can possibly be a true Christian, or a credit to his own religious society." In other words, a true Christian was one who possessed moral restraint that blessed the society through good citizenship and brought credibility to his own religious community as well. Washington was, in essence, applying the biblical teachings of James 2 to the spiritual and civil context: "Faith without works is dead."

If this was not a conversation between a group of Christians and a Christian president, then consider the incongruity that occurred here. A committee of preeminent theologians and elders representing their entire denomination were utterly deceived about Washington's faith. And Washington, unwilling to disabuse them of their mistaken notion, played along. Instead of honorably explaining their misunderstanding of his views, he furthered the mistake of the misguided Christian clergymen by deceptively expressing a faith he did not possess. Then to add insult to injury, he went on to expound as a false Christian a fundamental question of the Christian religion, namely, who is a true Christian. In so doing he, in essence, alluded to the teaching of the classic biblical text of James 2, which he, as a deist, did not believe.

Either Washington was a Christian, or he was a deceptive deist. If he were the latter, his claim to be a man of honesty and character—the very thing the Presbyterians had celebrated in their letter to Washington—was just as much a sham as his counterfeit Christianity and his pretense of piety.

### (7) George Washington's Sacred Fire

Hopefully we can now understand the interconnection between Washington's first inaugural address on April 30, 1789, and his first thanksgiving proclamation of October 3, 1789. In the first, he spoke of the "sacred fire of liberty" that had been entrusted to the American people in their "experiment" in representative government. In the second, he told the new nation how to fan the "sacred fire of liberty" so that it might burn even more brightly. His proposed method was by acknowledging the providence of almighty God and humbly imploring his blessing on the nation. Such words would have been most appropriate coming from the lips of a chaplain or a preacher from his pulpit. Yet it is striking just how naturally they came from George Washington as he assumed his pulpit of the presidency as America's first godly leader. Washington had indeed "turned preacher" after all.[116]

chapter 10

# CONCLUSION

*The first prayer in congress, September, 1774*

To continue our republic of freedom, we must stand boldly for our heritage. The proverbial frog in the slowly heating pot of water that is gradually cooked before he knows what has happened is the disconcerting reality of our nation and our nation's spiritual leaders. James Madison was surely describing our generation when he declared: "Since the general civilization of mankind, I believe there are more instances of the abridgment of the freedom of the people, by gradual and silent encroachments of those in power, than by violent and sudden usurpations."[117]

In 1776, patriotic visionary and writer Thomas Paine wrote a book entitled *Common Sense*. In that work, that galvanized the disparate colonies into a potent union of states acting against the tyranny of unbridled power in the face of the unjust usurpation of human rights, Paine proclaimed,

> The Sun never shined on a cause of greater worth. 'Tis not the affair of a City, a County, a Province or a Kingdom; but of a Continent...'Tis not the concern of a day, a year, or an age; posterity are virtually involved in the contest, and will be more or less affected even to the end of time by the proceedings now. Now is the seed time of Continental union, faith, and honour. The least

fracture now, will be like a name engraved with the point of a pin on the tender rind of a young oak; the wound will enlarge with the tree, and posterity read it in full grown characters.

What Paine said here came only weeks before our founders unanimously declared their independence on July 4th and is relevant for this discussion.

What I am calling you and others to do through the work of The Providence Forum is to reflect the commitment modeled by the Continental Congress. They consistently and self-consciously conceived of their role as defenders and preservers of the costly gift of religious and civil liberty:

> THAT it is an indispensable duty which we owe to God, our country, ourselves and posterity, by all lawful ways and means in our power to maintain, defend and preserve these civil and religious rights and liberties for which many of our fathers fought, bled and died, and to hand them down entire to future generations. (Journal of the Continental Congress, 1774, 32)

To accomplish such a great task, we clearly need the tenacious commitment to liberty articulated by President John F. Kennedy on January 20, 1961:

> Let every nation know, whether it wishes us well or ill, that we shall pay any price, bear any burden, meet any hardship, support any friend, oppose any foe to assure the survival and success of liberty.... The energy, the faith, the devotion which we bring to this endeavor will light our country and all who serve it—and the glow from that fire can truly light the world. And

*President John F. Kennedy – "...here on earth God's work must truly be our own."*

so, my fellow Americans, ask not what your country can do for you, ask what you can do for your country. With a good conscience our only sure reward, with history the final judge of our deeds, let us go forth to lead the land we love, asking His blessing and His help but knowing that here on earth God's work must truly be our own.*

To fulfill such a goal, we must also emulate the passion for liberty contained in the wisdom of Madison:

The nation which reposes on the pillow of political confidence, will sooner or later end its political existence in a deadly lethargy. (James Madison, Virginia Assembly, January 23, 1799)

Liberty and order will never be perfectly safe, until a trespass on the constitutional provision for either, shall be felt with the same keenness that resents an invasion of the dearest rights, until every citizen shall be an Argus to espy, and an Aegeon to avenge, the unhallowed deed. (James Madison, *National Gazette*, January 19, 1792)

And to the uncommon love of liberty found in Madison and Kennedy, and to the uncommon courage of our founding fathers, we must also not lose sight of that "common sense" American pluralism that affirms, "We are a religious people, and our Institutions presuppose a Supreme Being." This "Supreme Being" in the minds of our founders was none other than the Judeo-Christian God of what Washington called, "Holy Writ," "Scripture," and "the Word of God."

Thus, with full respect, I must conclude that your letter reveals that you may have:

1. Either lost sight of our nation's history, or consider it either deeply flawed or irrelevant.

2.  Unwittingly denied free speech to people of faith and to the views of our founding fathers.

3.  Accepted recent opinions and rulings of the High Court as though they are historically correct.

4.  Assumed that there can be a values neutral government.

5.  Overstated your commitment to a Christian worldview, or failed to understand it fully.

6.  Confused the complementary yet highly distinct functions of Gospel and culture.

7.  Affirmed that government is irrelevant to the legitimate advance of foundational concepts of a Judeo-Christian worldview.

8.  Compromised your understanding of a Christian worldview by accepting inconsistent tenets from secular thought, or what we have discovered to be historic anti-religion "liberalism."

Because so many consciously or unconsciously hold these views, the work of The Providence Forum must continue. As one of my friends has put it, "We as Americans have educated ourselves out of our heritage." As Franklin put it, we still, although precariously, have a republic, "if we can keep it." Our struggle for true liberty is still that of the whole world. As Franklin said famously in Paris in 1777, "It is the common observation here that our cause is the cause of all mankind, and that we are fighting for their liberty in defending our own."*

*President Abraham Lincoln*

If we truly desire a lasting republic with abiding liberty and justice for all, we must deeply ponder what Lincoln said in a speech from the early part of his career entitled, "The Perpetuation of Our Political Institutions." On January 27, 1838 in Springfield, Illinois, Lincoln asserted:

> At what point shall we expect the approach of danger? . . . Shall we expect some trans-Atlantic military giant to step the ocean and crush us at a blow? Never! All the armies of Europe, Asia and

Africa combined with all the treasure of the earth (our own excepted) in their military chest; with a Buonaparte for a commander, could not by force take a drink from the Ohio or make a track on the Blue Ridge, in a trial of a thousand years. At what point then is the approach of danger to be expected? If destruction be our lot, we must ourselves be its author and finisher. As a nation of free men, we must live through all time, or die by suicide.[118]

In the face of the truculent enemies of unbelief and secularism, there must be no ambivalence about our will to live as a Judeo-Christian culture. To hesitate here and to compromise now is tantamount to distributing the very poison that is causing the decay and ultimate death of our declining post-Judeo-Christian culture.

So I call on you in humility and sincerity to join me in an "appeal to the Supreme Judge of the world." To that appeal we must combine America's historic "common sense" belief in a "Supreme Being" with our founders' and patriots' Judeo-Christian uncommon love for liberty. Only then will we begin to portray President Kennedy's patriotic and passionate public promise,

> Let every nation know, whether it wishes us well or ill, that we shall pay any price, bear any burden, meet any hardship, support any friend, oppose any foe to assure the survival and the success of liberty.

I for one pledge to do the same, "So help me God."

# Epilogue

Ten Things Everyone Should Consider In Order To Impact The Public Square and To Redefine *The Wall Of Misconception:*

1. Get informed. Read broadly and listen to the media from several perspectives. Attend relevant conferences and seminars. No one group or vantage point gets all of the issues right.
2. Get involved. Register to vote. Study the candidates and the issues. Vote on election day. Encourage others to participate in the electoral process also. Volunteer and serve as able.
3. Get educated. Take a class or earn a degree in order to maximize your understanding of public policy, public service, governmental functions, or political process.
4. Care enough to pray for, to give to, or to serve organizations that advance the core values of your conscience.
5. Remember that true victory is won by truth, logic, facts, and persistence, not political intrigue, emotional outbursts, or acts of violence. Act according to this creed.
6. Be committed to the long haul, not the quick fix. The solution to America's problems in the relationship of church and state will take generations, not just a few weeks or a few elections.
7. Encourage your religious fellowship to organize and to conduct a voter's registration, an activity that is entirely appropriate for a non-profit organization.
8. Consider running for office, volunteering for a candidate who is seeking to advance the values of your conscience, serving on a volunteer public organization or board that helps to shape policy for your community, your political party, or your social or religious community.
9. Join The Providence Forum by regularly checking our website, receiving our newsletter and distributing our literature and books such as *The Wall of Misconception.*

10.  Write an op-ed piece for your local paper, newsletter or service group that highlights the critical cultural and moral issues of our day.

There are many more things you could do. Let these be a start to get you asking what you can do. Remember, all that is necessary for evil to triumph is for good men to do nothing! As Ronald Reagan once said, "If not this, what? If not now, when? If not me, who?"* May you be moved to be part of the solution and not part of the problem as we together seek to turn the wall of misconception back into the friendly wall of separation between church and state.

# Endnotes

1    An overview of Blackstone's view of law is available from The Providence Forum.

2    An overview of John Locke's views of God, government, and faith is available from The Providence Forum.

3    In his *magnum opus, An American Dictionary of the English Language* (1828), Noah Webster defined happy and happiness as follows: HAP'PINESS, n. [from happy.] The agreeable sensations which spring from the enjoyment of good; that state of a being in which his desires are gratified, by the enjoyment of pleasure without pain; felicity; but happiness usually expresses less than felicity, and felicity less than bliss. Happiness is comparative. To a person distressed with pain, relief from that pain affords happiness; in other cases we give the name happiness to positive pleasure or an excitement of agreeable sensations. Happiness therefore admits of indefinite degrees of increase in enjoyment, or gratification of desires. **Perfect happiness, or pleasure unalloyed with pain, is not attainable in this life**. 2. Good luck; good fortune. 3. Fortuitous elegance; unstudied grace. For there's a happiness as well as care.

HAP'PY a. [from hap.] 1. Lucky; fortunate; successful. Chemists have been more happy in finding experiments, than the causes of them. So we say, a happy thought; a happy expedient. 2. Being in the enjoyment of agreeable sensations from the possession of good; enjoying pleasure from the gratification of appetites or desires. **The pleasurable sensations derived from the gratification of sensual appetites render a person temporarily happy; but he only can be esteemed really and permanently happy, who enjoys peace of mind in the favor of God**. To be in any degree happy, we must be free from pain both of body and of mind; to be very happy, we must be in the enjoyment of lively sensations of pleasure, either of body or mind. Happy am I, for the daughters will call me blessed. (Gen.30) He found himself happiest, in communicating happiness to others. 3. **Prosperous; having secure possession of good. Happy is that people whose God is Jehovah**. (Ps.144) 4. That supplies pleasure; that furnishes enjoyment; agreeable; applied to things; as a happy condition. 5. Dexterous; ready; able. One gentleman is happy at a reply, another excels in a rejoinder. 6. **Blessed; enjoying the presence and favor of God, in a future life**. 7. Harmonious; living in concord; enjoying the pleasures of friendship; as a happy family. 8. Propitious; favorable. (emphasis added)

4    Samuel Adam's emphasis upon Christ's Kingship reflects the spirit of Massachusetts and the other colonies of his day. Statements such as these became commonplace: "No King but King Jesus!" (a slogan emanating from the Committees of Correspondence). A crown appointed governor to the Board of Trade in England wrote, "If you ask an American, who is his master? He will tell you he has none, nor any governor but Jesus Christ." This needs a bit of explanation. The English colonialists were not inherently opposed to monarchy per se. But King George had, in the minds of many colonialists, usurped the rule of Christ in his actions toward New England. The third charge of The Declaration of Independence against the King says, "He has refused to pass other laws for the accommodation of large districts of people unless those people would relinquish the right of representation in the legislature, a right inestimable to them and formidable to tyrants only." Charge XX says, "For abolishing the free system of English laws in a neighboring province, establishing therein an arbitrary government, and enlarging its boundaries, so as to render it at once an example and fit instrument for introducing the same absolute rule into these colonies." The issue involved in both of these charges is the loss of the British form of government in favor of a French variety and the establishment of the Roman Catholic religion in Quebec. The vast majority of the people in Quebec were Roman Catholic, but the government had been English. But by the Quebec Act British law was set aside and the Roman Catholic religion established. There were those who believed these concessions to the Canadian Roman Catholics were made so that the British army would have a friendly staging area for an invasion of the colonies if the struggle with the crown came to blows. The Continental Congress declared, "that the late act of Parliament for establishing the Roman Catholic religion and the French laws in that extensive country now called Quebec, is dangerous in an extreme degree to the Protestant religion and to the civil rights and liberties of all America; and therefore as men and protestant Christians, we are indispensably obliged to take all proper measures for our security." (*Journal of the*

*Proceedings of Congress*, Sept. 17, 1774, p. 35.); and again, "establishing an absolute Government and the Roman Catholic Religion throughout those vast regions, that border on the westerly and northerly boundaries of the free, protestant English settlements." (p. 138). It should not be thought, however, that the American colonies had no room for Roman Catholics in their lands. This was made clear by General Washington's instructions to Benedict Arnold (not then viewed as a traitor) prior to the American invasion of Canada. Washington said to Arnold, "I also give it in Charge to you to avoid all Disrespect to or Contempt of the Religion of the Country and its Ceremonies. Prudence, Policy, and a true Christian Spirit, will lead us to look with Compassion upon their Errors without insulting them...God alone is the Judge of the Hearts of Men, and to him only in the Case, they are answerable." (*Writings of George Washington*, Vol., p. 492.) Consider also the Continental Congress' letter to the Roman Catholic citizens of Quebec. The Continental Congress wrote, "We are too well acquainted with the liberality of sentiment distinguishing your nation, to imagine, that difference of religion will prejudice you against a hearty amity with us. You know, that the transcendent nature of freedom elevates those, who unite in her cause, above all such low minded infirmities. The Swiss Cantons furnish a memorable proof of this truth. Their union is composed of Roman Catholic and Protestant States, living in the utmost concord and peace with one another, and thereby enabled, ever since they bravely vindicated their freedom, to defy and defeat every tyrant that has invaded them." ( p. 129). The Articles of Confederation, the first form of government for the United States before our Constitution, provided for the annexation of Canada! *The bottom line is that the Revolutionary War was in part a religious war.* The Americans called themselves "protestants," "ancient free protestant colonies," "free, protestant, English settlements" (p. 138.), etc. Nevertheless, there was a hope to have a peaceful co-existence with Roman Catholics.

5    Please see my book entitled, *Proclaim Liberty.... A Broken Bell Rings Freedom to the World* (Providence Forum, 2001) that develops this theme.

6    A summary of the empirical evidence of our founders' substantial dependence on Judeo-Christian thought emerging from the Bible is available from The Providence Forum.

7    This testimony in full is available from The Providence Forum

8    This was given at their request on the sixty-first anniversary of the Declaration of Independence, July 4, 1837.

9    U.S. Supreme Court, 1891, *Church of the Holy Trinity v. The United States.*

10    If you are interested in pursuing this more fully, please request from The Providence Forum a copy of the "Expert Testimony" paper I prepared for the Chester County Federal court case concerning the Ten Commandments Plaque on the courthouse wall.

11    A summary of the importance of Penn's efforts for religious freedom is outlined on pages 16-24 of *Proclaim Liberty*, published by The Providence Forum.

12    See *The Papers of George Washington: The Presidential Series* ed. Dorothy Twohig, (Charlottesville: University Press of Virginia, 1996), 6:284-85. This was written on August 17, 1790. See also Washington's letter to the Hebrew Congregation in Savannah, Georgia, May 1790, in *The Papers of George Washington*, 5:448-449. There he writes, "I rejoice that a spirit of liberality and philanthropy is much more prevalent than it formerly was among the enlightened nations of the earth; and that your brethren will benefit thereby in proportion as it shall become still more extensive. Happily the people of the United Sates of America have, in many instances, exhibited examples worthy of imitation—The salutary influence of which will doubtless extend much farther; if gratefully enjoying those blessings of peace which (under favor of Heaven) have been obtained by fortitude in war, they shall conduct themselves with reverence to the Deity, and charity towards their fellow-creatures. May the same wonder-working Deity, who long since delivering the Hebrews from their Egyptian Oppressors planted them in the promised land—whose providential agency has lately been conspicuous in establishing these United States as an independent nation—still continue to water them with the dews of Heaven and to make the inhabitants of every denomination participate in the temporal and spiritual blessings of that people whose God is Jehovah." James Madison wrote to Mordecai M. Noah, May 15, 1818, "Having ever regarded the freedom of religious opinions & worship as equally belonging to every sect, & the secure enjoyment of it as the best human provision for bringing all either into the same way of thinking, or into that mutual charity which is the only substitute, I observe with pleasure the view you give of the spirit of which your Sect [Jewish] partake of the blessings offered by our Government and Laws." To Jacob de la Motta, he wrote in August

1820, "The history of the Jews must forever be interesting. The modern part of it is, at the same time so little generally known, that every ray of light of the subject has its value. Among the features peculiar to the Political system of the U. States, is the perfect equality of rights which it secures to every religious Sect. And it is particularly pleasing to observe in the good citizenship of such as have been most distrusted and oppressed elsewhere, a happy illustration of the safety & success of this experiment of a just & benignant policy. Equal laws protecting equal rights, are found as they ought to be presumed, the best guarantee of loyalty & love of country; as well as best calculated to cherish that mutual respect & good will among Citizens of every religious denomination which are necessary to social harmony and most favorable to the advancement of truth. The account you give of the Jews of your congregation brings them fully within the scope of these observations." Padover, *The Complete Madison*, p. 310-11.

13    This perspective was that of the Adams household. Around November 5, 1775, Abigail Adams wrote to her friend, Mercy Warren:

A patriot without religion in my estimation is as great a paradox as an honest Man without the fear of God. Is it possible that he whom no moral obligations bind, can have any real Good Will towards Men? Can he be a patriot who, by an openly vicious conduct, is undermining the very bonds of Society?...The Scriptures tell us "righteousness exalteth a Nation." Regarding his sons, John Adams advised his wife, Abigail to: "Let them revere nothing but Religion, Morality and Liberty."

14    George F. Hoar is quoted in *Old South Leaflets*. No. 13, p. 11 as follows, "The Ordinance of 1787 belongs with the Declaration of Independence and the Constitution. It is one of the three title deeds of American constitutional liberty. As the American youth for uncounted centuries shall visit the capital of his country. . . if he knew his country's history, and considered wisely the sources of her glory, there is nothing in all these which will so stir his heart as two faded and time-soiled papers, whose characters were traced by the hand of the fathers a hundred years ago. They are the original records of the acts which devoted this nation forever to equality, to education, to religion and to liberty. One is the Declaration of Independence, the other the Ordinance of 1787."

15    See above for a discussion of Madison's views of faith.

16    Quoted in *The New Dictionary of Thoughts*. New York: Standard Book, Co. 1949, p. 337.

17    There was a very close personal connection between Madison and Jefferson. See Padover, *The Complete Madison*, p. 6-11.

18    William R. Estep, *Revolution within the Revolution The First Amendment in the Historical Context 1612-1789* (Grand Rapids Michigan: William B. Eerdmans Publishing Company, 1990) p. 194-195. Patrick Henry also had a significant impact on religious liberty in Virginia as well. In what became known as "The Parson's Cause," he helped defeat the required payment of tithes to the state church by the citizens of Virginia, a law that forced many to support a church they did not believe in. Eidsmoe writes, "Several Anglican clergymen were suing some tobacco planters under a Virginia colony law that required a certain portion of tobacco revenues be paid for the support of the clergy. Henry agreed to defend the planters when their previous attorney declared the case hopeless and withdrew. He assailed the Anglican clergy without mercy, amid a packed courtroom filled with Anglican clergymen confident of victory, and 'Dissenters' (Methodists, Baptists, and Presbyterians) looking to Henry as their champion: 'We have heard a great deal about the benevolence and holy zeal of our reverend clergy, but how is this manifested? Do they manifest their zeal in the cause of religion and humanity by practicing the mild and benevolent precepts of the Gospel of Jesus? Do they feed the hungry and clothe the naked? Oh, no, gentlemen! Instead of feeding the hungry and clothing the naked, these rapacious harpies would, were their powers equal to their will, snatch from the hearth of their honest parishioner his last hoe-cake, from the widow and her orphan children their last milch cow! The last bed, nay, the last blanket from the lying-in woman!' Henry could not demand a verdict for the planters since the law was clearly on the side of the clergy. Instead, he asked the jury to bring forth a verdict for the clergy in the amount of one penny—which the jury did." John Eidsmoe, *Christianity and the Constitution*, (Grand Rapids: Baker Book House, 1987), p. 301. Henry also helped to defend persecuted preachers of the Gospel who were not part of the established church. William J. Federer writes, "Prior to the Revolution, in 1768, Patrick Henry rode for miles on horseback to a trial in Spottsylvania county. He entered the rear of a courtroom where three Baptist ministers were being

tried for having preached without the sanction of the Episcopalian Church. In the midst of the proceedings, he interrupted: "May it please your lordships, what did I hear read? Did I hear an expression that these men, whom you worships are about to try for misdemeanor, are charged with preaching the gospel of the Son of God?"' In William J. Federer, *America's God and Country* (Coppel, Texas: Fame Publishing, Inc., 1994), p. 287.

19    In Estep, *Revolution within the Revolution*, p. 201.

20    1. Congress shall make no laws touching religion, or to infringe the rights of conscience. (6/21/1788)

2. That religion, or the duty which we owe to our creator, and the manner of discharging it, can be directed only by reason and conviction, not by force or violence, and therefore all men have an equal, natural and unalienable right to the free exercise of religion according to the dictates of conscience, and that no particularly religious sect or society ought to be favored or established by law in preference to others. (6/26/1788)

3. That the people have an equal, natural, and unalienable right freely and peaceably to exercise their religion, according to the dictates of conscience; and that no religious sect or society ought to be favored or established by law in preference to others. (7/26/1788)

4. That any person religiously scrupulous of bearing arms ought to be exempted, upon payment of an equivalent to employ another to bear arms in his stead. (8/1/1788) (this clause added to the above)

5. The civil rights of none shall be abridged on account of religious belief or worship, nor shall any national religion be established, nor shall the full and equal rights of conscience be in any manner, or any pretext infringed. (6/8/1789 as part of James Madison's initial draft for a Bill of Rights)

6. No state shall violate the equal right of conscience, or the freedom of the press, or the trial by jury in criminal cases. (6/8/1789—as part of James Madison's initial draft for a Bill of Rights)

The following three clauses were presented in an initial draft of the Bill of Rights, drafted by a committee of eleven representatives duly appointed by the House following Madison's urging:

7. No religion shall be established by law, nor shall the equal rights of conscience be infringed (7/28/1789)

8. No person religiously scrupulous shall be compelled to bear arms

9. No State shall infringe the equal rights of conscience, nor the freedom of speech or of the press, nor of the right of trial by jury in criminal cases.

Additional iterations:

10. Congress shall make no laws touching religion or infringing the rights of conscience.

11. The equal rights of conscience, the freedom of speech or of the press, and the right of trial by jury in criminal cases, shall not be infringed by any State.

12. Congress shall make no law establishing religion, or to prevent the free exercise thereof, or to infringe the rights of conscience.

13. No person religiously scrupulous shall be compelled to bear arms in person.

14. Congress shall make no law establishing religion, or prohibiting the free exercise thereof, nor shall the rights of conscience be infringed.

15. Congress shall make no law establishing One Religious sect or Society in preference to others, nor shall the rights of conscience be infringed.

16. Congress shall not make any law, infringing the rights of conscience, or establishing any Religious Sect or Society.

17. Congress shall make no law establishing any particular denomination of religion in preference to another, or prohibiting the free exercise thereof, nor shall the rights of conscience be infringed.

18. Congress shall make no law establishing religion, or prohibiting the free exercise thereof.

19. Congress shall make no law establishing articles of faith or a mode of worship, or prohibiting the free exercise of religion, or abridging the freedom of speech, or the press, or the right of the people peaceably to assemble, and petition to the Government for the redress of grievances. (9/9/1789)

20. Congress shall make no Law respecting an establishment of Religion, or prohibiting the free exercise thereof. (9/24/1789). See John Witte Jr., *Religion and the American Constitutional Experiment* (Boulder, Colorado: Westview Press, 2000), p. 64-72.

21    Similarly in his letter to the members of the Baltimore Baptist Association, October 17, 1808, he writes:

"In our early struggles for liberty, religious freedom could not fail to become a primary object. All men felt the right, and a just animation to obtain it was exhibited by all. I was one only among the many who befriended its establishment, and am entitled but in common with others to a portion of that approbation which follows the fulfillment of a duty.

Excited by wrongs to reject a foreign government which directed our concerns according to its own interests, and not to ours, the principles which justified us were obvious to all understandings, they were imprinted in the breast of every human being; and Providence ever pleases to direct the issue of our contest in favor of that side where justice was. Since this happy separation, our nation has wisely avoided entangling itself in the system of European interests, has taken no side between its rival powers, attached itself to none of its ever-changing confederacies. Their peace is desirable; and you do me justice in saying that to preserve and secure this has been the constant aim of my administration. The difficulties which involve it, however, are now at their ultimate term, and what will be their issue, time alone will disclose. But be it what it may, a recollection of our former vassalage in religion and civil government, will unite the zeal of every heart, and the energy of every hand, to preserve that independence in both which, under the favor of heaven, a disinterested devotion to the public cause first achieved, and a disinterested sacrifice of private interests will now maintain."

22  As an example of a church that changed its creed in the context of the American experience of religious liberty, note the striking difference in understanding of the relationship of church and state between the original version of the Presbyterian *Westminster Confession of Faith*, and the altered American text. The original version of 1647 affirms that the magistrate ought to have the coercive power in religious matters.

"The civil magistrate may not assume to himself the administration of the Word and sacraments, or the power of the keys of the kingdom of heaven; yet he hath authority, and it is his duty, to take order that unity and peace be preserved in the Church, that the truth of God be kept pure and entire, that all blasphemies and heresies be suppressed, all corruptions and abuses in worship and discipline prevented or reformed, and all the ordinances of God duly settled, administered, and observed. For the better effecting whereof, he hath power to call synods, to be present at them and to provide that whatsoever is transacted in them be according to the mind of God." (XXIII. 3)

Under the leadership of John Witherspoon, the president of Princeton, and the only clergyman to sign the Declaration of Independence, the Presbyterian Church in the United States amended its *Confession*. The American Edition of the *Confession*, thus adopted in 1789, recognized a clear distinction between the power of the state and the power of the church, noting that the government should protect all faiths, not just one established religion. Chapter XXIII. 3 states:

"Civil magistrates may not assume to themselves the administration of the Word and sacraments; or the power of the keys of the kingdom of heaven; or, in the least, interfere in matters of faith. Yet, as nursing fathers, it is the duty of civil magistrates to protect the Church of our common Lord, without giving the preference to any denomination of Christians above the rest, in such a manner that all ecclesiastical persons whatever shall enjoy the full, free, and unquestioned liberty of discharging every part of their sacred functions, without violence or danger. And, as Jesus Christ hath appointed a regular government and discipline in his Church, no law of any commonwealth should interfere with, let, or hinder, the due exercise thereof, among the voluntary members of any denomination of Christians, according to their own profession and belief. It is the duty of civil magistrates to protect the person and good name of all their people, in such an effectual manner as that no person be suffered, either upon pretense of religion or of infidelity, to offer any indignity, violence, abuse, or injury to any other person whatsoever: and to take order, that all religious and ecclesiastical assemblies be held without molestation or disturbance."

23  It is interesting to observe the gradual change in the Pennsylvania Constitution as it developed through the years. In June 18-25, 1776 the Provincial Conference of Committees of the Province of Pennsylvania met to discuss the issue of independence. It required the following religious test for those who would represent Pennsylvania at the Continental Congress:

"Resolved, That no Person elected to serve as a Member of Convention, shall take his seat or give his vote until he shall have made and subscribed to the following Declaration:

I _____ do profess faith in God the Father, and in Jesus Christ his eternal son, the true God, and in the Holy Spirit, one God Blessed for evermore; and do acknowledge the Holy Scriptures of the Old and New Testament to be given by Divine Inspiration." (See Proceedings of the Provincial Conference of Committees of the Province of Pennsylvania Held at Carpenters' Hall, Philadelphia June 18-25, 1776, Facsimile of an Original as printed by W. and T. Bradford. [Philadelphia: Independence Hall Association, 1989], p. 10.) This profession of faith was thus taken by Benjamin Franklin, who was a representative of Pennsylvania at the Provincial Conference of Committees.

Upon the adoption of the Declaration of Independence, the Pennsylvania Assembly wrote its new constitution. The Pennsylvania Constitution continues to require a similar test of faith but one that is not explicitly Trinitarian:

And each member, before he takes his seat, shall make and subscribe the following declaration, viz:

"I do believe in one God, the creator and governor of the universe, the rewarder of the good and the punisher of the wicked. And I do acknowledge the Scriptures of the Old and New Testament to be given by Divine inspiration."

In the 1791 version of the Pennsylvania Constitution, (after the adoption of the First Amendment of the Bill of Rights) this religious test was removed. From the 1776 Pennsylvania Constitution until today, the rights of conscience have been guaranteed. The language of the 1776 Constitution begins, even as Penn's *Charter* did, with the emphasis on religious liberty:

"A DECLARATION OF THE RIGHTS OF THE INHABITANTS
OF THE COMMONWEALTH OR STATE OF PENNSYLVANIA

I. That all men are born equally free and independent, and have certain natural, inherent and unalienable rights, amongst which are, the enjoying and defending life and liberty, acquiring, possessing and protecting property, and pursuing and obtaining happiness and safety.

II. That all men have a natural and unalienable right to worship Almighty God according to the dictates of their own consciences and understanding: And that no man ought or of right can be compelled to attend any religious worship, or erect or support any place of worship, or maintain any ministry, contrary to, or against, his own free will and consent: Nor can any man, who acknowledges the being of a God, be justly deprived or abridged of any civil right as a citizen, on account of his religious sentiments or peculiar mode of religious worship: And that no authority can or ought to be vested in, or assumed by any power whatever, that shall in any case interfere with, or in any manner controul, the right of conscience in the free exercise of religious worship."

In the Pennsylvania Constitution of 1790, the same language in defense of the rights on conscience is found in Article IX:

"Article IX,

That all men have a natural and indefeasible right to worship Almighty God according to the dictates of their own consciences; that no man can of right be compelled to attend, erect, or support any place of worship, or to maintain any ministry, against his consent; that no human authority can, in any case whatever, control or interfere with the rights of conscience; and that no preference shall ever be given, by law, to any religious establishment or modes of worship.

Article IX, Sec. 4. That no person, who acknowledges the being of a God and a future state of rewards and punishments, shall, on account of his religious sentiments, be disqualified to hold any office or place of trust or profit under this commonwealth."

*Section 4* cited immediately above, in its original intent, protected the person that did not conform to the prevailing theological views of the day. Since this language continues to this day, it now has the effect of protecting the person of faith from an atheistic, secular interpretation of secular government. Either way, then and now, the Constitution has preserved and continues to preserve the rights of conscience.

For the above texts, see *http://www.yale.edu/lawweb/avalon/avalon.htm*

24  Starting with the Bolshevik rise to power in 1917, followed by the Communist regime under Stalin and Khrushchev, until the fall of the Berlin Wall, the church and religion in the Soviet Union suffered an unending barrage of attacks on the structural and ideological underpinnings of the church. Legal and propaganda attacks

destroyed the infrastructure of the church and credibility and status of the clergy. The infamous Stalin purges successfully decimated the ranks of the clergy, as well as religious institutions, and houses of worship. In spite of Khrushchev's statements that the Soviet Union continued to support "full freedom of conscience and religion", the reality was far different. Perhaps truer to the communist view of liberty is the quote attributed to Vladimir Ilyich Lenin, "It is true that liberty is precious—so precious that it must be rationed." Attributed and quoted by Sidney and Beatrice Webb, *Soviet Communism: A New Civilization?* (1936), p. 1036.

25  As we have already noted, The Declaration of Independence has four references to God.

26  Our money bears the inscription, "In God we trust" which was the last official act signed into law by Lincoln before he was assassinated. On April 24, 1865, Schuyler Colfax, the Speaker of the House of Representatives, stated in a Memorial Address for President Lincoln, "Nor should I forget to mention here that the last act of Congress ever signed by him was one requiring that the motto, in which he sincerely believed, 'In God We Trust,' should hereafter be inscribed upon all our national coin."

Our national motto was actually first proposed in the poem that would become our national anthem, which was born out of the War of 1812. The story begins with the first light of dawn on September 13, 1814. It was then that the British fleet commenced its bombardment of Fort McHenry in Baltimore's harbor. Throughout the day and night the cannonade continued lighting up the sky with explosions.

Aboard a British ship, as the battle ensued, were two Americans under a flag of truce. Francis Scott Key and the other man were there to negotiate an exchange of prisoners. During the bombing, Key wrote in his notebook the words that came to mind as he watched to see if the fort's huge flag was still standing after each blast. Early on the next day, a storm blew in, shrouding the attack on Baltimore's harbor. Key hoped to see the star spangled banner still flying over Fort McHenry. Joyfully, at the first light of dawn, he saw the American flag still waving over the Fort. It was then that he wrote the moving poem that would become our national anthem:

*The National Anthem*

O say, can you see, by the dawn's early light,
What so proudly we hailed at the twilight's last gleaming,
Whose broad stripes and bright stars, through the perilous fight,
O'er the ramparts we watched, were so gallantly streaming?
And the rockets' red glare, the bombs bursting in air,
Gave proof through the night that our flag was still there.
O say, does that star spangled banner yet wave
O'er the land of the free and the home of the brave?

O thus be it ever, when free men shall stand
Between their loved homes and the war's desolation!
Blest with vict'ry and peace, may the heav'n-rescued land
Praise the Pow'r that hath made and preserved us a nation!
Then conquer we must, when our cause it is just;
And this be our motto: In God is our trust!"
And the star-spangled banner in triumph shall wave
O'er the land of the free and the home of the brave!

The last stanza suggests our motto and affirms a theistic perspective.

27  The Latin phrase "*Annuit Coeptis*" can be found on the back of the U. S. One Dollar Bill. It was added to the Great Seal of the United States by Continental Congress Secretary Charles Thompson. A classics and biblical scholar, Thompson took the phrase from Virgil. It means "He has smiled (nodded) on our undertakings." It communicates the belief that God's providence had blessed America's struggle for freedom. Consider the explanation of the Great Seal of the U. S. given in the Journal of the Continental Congress:

"REVERSE. A pyramid unfinished. In the zenith, an eye in a triangle, surrounded with a glory proper. Over the eye these words, Annuit Coeptis. On the base of the pyramid the numerical letters

MDCCLXXVI. And underneath the following motto, *Novus Ordo Seclorum*. . .

Reverse: The Pyramid signifies strength and duration. The eye over it and the motto allude to the many signal interpositions of providence in favour of the American cause. The date underneath is that of the Declaration of Independence, and the words under it signify the beginning of the new American Era, which commences from that date..." (Vol XXII). The history of the seal is told in the Journal of the Continental Congress. This shows that the "eye of providence" was a basic idea from the very first design of the seal dating to 1776. The symbol of the eye of Providence in a triangle is a Christian Trinitarian symbol depicting God the Father as the agent of sovereign providence in history.

28    The historical details of the Pledge of Allegiance were discussed above.

29    Philip Wogaman, *Christian Perspectives on Politics*, (London: SCM, 1988), p. 188.

30    The architecture of the Supreme Court Building: reflects the centrality of The Ten Commandments in several ways:

"This room has four marble bas-relief panels beneath the ceiling on each of the four walls. The panel directly above the bench where the Chief Justice and Eight associate Justices are seated depicts "The Power of Government" and "The Majesty of the Law." Between these two allegorical figures are the Ten Commandments. One gains access to the inner courtroom through an oak doorway. Each door has engraved upon its lower half the Ten Commandments. Above the inscription "Justice, the Guardian of Liberty" portrays Moses in the center with the two tablets of the LAW, the Ten Commandments, in either hand. This is a stark reminder of the origin and basis for our American legal system." Source: Catherine Millard, *God's Signature over the Nation's Capitol*.

31    Quoted in the *New Dictionary of Thoughts*, New York: Standard Book Co., 1949, p. 32.

32    Jefferson said this in the context of the early acceptance of slavery in America.

33    *The Universal Declaration of Human Rights*, adopted by the United Nations on December 10, 1948, states: "Everyone has the right to freedom of thought, conscience and religion; this right includes freedom to change his religion or belief, and freedom, either alone or in community with others and in public or private, to manifest his religion or belief in teaching, practice, worship and observance."

34    The American notion of liberty in law is well reflected in President Franklin D. Roosevelt's address to the US Congress on January 6, 1941. He said, "In the future days which we seek to make secure, we look forward to a world founded upon four essential human freedoms. The first is freedom of speech and expression—everywhere in the world. The second is freedom of every person to worship God in his own way—everywhere in the world. The third is freedom from want—which, translated into world terms, means economic undertakings which will secure to every nation a healthy peacetime life for its inhabitants—everywhere in the world. The fourth is freedom from fear—which, translated into world terms, means a worldwide reduction of armaments to such a point and in such a thorough fashion that no nation will be in a position to commit an act of physical aggression against any neighbor—anywhere in the world. . . Freedom means the supremacy of human rights everywhere."

35    According to Adrian Karatnycky of Freedom House, "The correlation between Christianity and freedom at the end of the twentieth century is very strong...Christian countries, at this stage of human development, are about six times more likely to be free and democratic, as they are to be non-democratic and suffer from serious abridgements in human rights." (Adrian Karatnycky, "Religious Freedom and the New Millennium" given at the International Coalition for Religious Freedom Conference on "Religious Freedom and the New Millennium" in Berlin Germany, May 29-31, 1998, p. 111.) Further, "Of the 81 countries that we rate as free in our survey, 74 are majority Christian. Of the seven free countries that are not majority Christian, one is Israel, which is part of the Judeo-Christian civilization. Two others, Mauritius and South Korea, have very large Christian communities, and in some cases growing Christian communities, more than a third of their population. Of the four free countries that don't have strong relations to the Judeo-Christian tradition, one is Mali, which is predominately Muslim. Another is Taiwan, where nearly half the population is Buddhist. Another is Mongolia, which is traditional Buddhist. And finally there is Japan, which observes both the Buddhist and Shinto traditions." (Adrian Karatnycky, "The Changing Landscape of Religious Freedom", given at the International Coalition of Religious Freedom Conference on "Religious Freedom in Latin America and

the New Millennium" October 10-12, 1998 in San Paolo, Brazil.) www.icrf.com. There is also an historic commitment of religious toleration in Buddhism. Ninan Koshy writes in *Religious Freedom in a Changing World*, Risk Books Series, (Geneva: WCC Publications, 1992), p. 51 writes, "Twenty-three centuries ago King Ashoka, patron of Buddhism, recommended to his subjects that they should act in accordance with a principle of toleration. 'Acting thus, we contribute to our creed by serving other. Acting otherwise, we harm our own faith, bringing discredit upon the others. He who exalts his own belief, discrediting all others does so surely to obey his religion with the intention of making a display of it. But behaving thus, he gives it the hardest blows. And for this reason concord is good only in so far as all listen to each other's creeds and live to listen to them.'"

36  A vision statement for the growth of Islam in America is found in note #43 below.

37  The speech by President George W. Bush given May 7, 2001, to the American Jewish Committee entitled, "The First Freedom of the Soul," I quote these relevant portions:

"crimes are being committed today by the government of Sudan, which is waging war against that country's traditionalist and Christian peoples. Some 2 million Sudanese have lost their lives; 4 million more have lost their homes. Hospitals, schools, churches and international relief stations have often been bombed by government warplanes over the 18 years of Sudan's civil war. The government claims to have halted air attacks. But they continue. Women and children have been abducted and sold into slavery. UNICEF estimates that some 12,000 to 15,000 people are now held in bondage in Sudan.

The story of the Exodus still speaks across the millennium; no society in all of history can be justly built on the backs of slaves. Sudan is a disaster area for human rights. The right of conscience has been singled out for special abuse by the Sudanese authorities. Aid agencies report that food assistance is sometimes distributed only to those willing to undergo conversion to Islam. . . .

I'm pleased to say that many countries in the region show considerable and improving respect for religious liberty: Morocco, Tunisia, Jordan and Bahrain among them. But there are other regimes, not only in North Africa and the Middle East, whose disrespect for freedom of worship is seriously disturbing.

Iraq murders dissident religious figures. Iran systematically maltreats Jews, Christians and adherents of the Baha'i faith. The Burmese junta tortures adherents of Islam, Buddhism and Christianity. Cuba monitors and harasses independent priests and ministers. Afghanistan's Taliban government has horrified the world with its disdain for fundamental human freedoms, epitomized by its destruction of ancient Buddhist works of art. And the newly independent republics of Central Asia impose troubling limits on religious expression and missionary work."

38  See A Summary of Findings Based on 2000 Annual Report on International Religious Freedom, Issued By The Bureau of Democracy, Human Rights, and Labor, U. S. Department of State, 5 September 2000 in *Proclaim Liberty: . . . A Broken Bell Rings Freedom to the World* by Peter A. Lillback (Bryn Mawr: The Providence Forum, 2001), p. 59. Several of these countries fall in the categories of regimes that display overt hostility toward minority religions, or discrimination and persecution toward minority religions either through legislation or stigmatization through association.

39  America's national freedom, which began on July 4, 1776, and was first publicly proclaimed on July 8, 1776, was given birth by a courageous band of colonists assembled in Philadelphia. They had a vision for a nation with a new form of government, free from tyranny. The new millennium marks the 225th anniversary of their declaration that gave us our legacy of American liberty and independence.

But this great event in the annals of human freedom had an important historical context. The Liberty Bell, which announced the arrival of American independence, had itself been ordered in 1751 to commemorate a milestone on the path to liberty. This was a charter that was crafted three hundred years ago on October 28, 1701, seventy-five years before our Declaration of Independence was written. It was then that William Penn (1644-1718), the sole proprietor of a vast land grant from King Charles II of England (1630-1685), gave to the new world one of the greatest liberties mankind has ever known—the freedom to worship God according to the dictates of one's own conscience. In our age of religious diversity and political pluralism, we can easily slip into complacency regarding this freedom that Penn put *first* in his *Charter of Privileges*. William Penn wrote: "I doe hereby Grant and Declare that noe person or persons Inhabiting in this Province or Territories who shall Confesse and Acknowledge one Almighty God the Creator upholder and Ruler of the world and professe him or themselves Obliged to live quietly under the Civill Government shall be in any case molested or prejudiced in his or theire person or Estate because of his or theire Conscientious perswasion or practice nor be compelled to frequent or mentaine any Religious Worship place or Ministry contrary to his or theire mind or doe or Suffer any other act or thing contrary to theire Religious perswasion."

Religious liberty is today understood to be a "right" of every American citizen as guaranteed in our Bill of Rights. The First Amendment declares, "Congress shall make no law respecting an establishment of religion, or prohibiting the free exercise thereof." Yet this right of religious liberty was not easy to attain, nor has it been simple to maintain. Indeed, Penn's vision for a free society with freedom of religious conscience was conceived in the Tower of London where Penn was imprisoned for his Quaker convictions. This cardinal principle of religious liberty granted by Penn's Charter established a most important constitutional precedent. When this principle was later encoded in the United States Constitution, it made America unique among the nations of the earth. Indeed, millions of people around the globe still do not have this most basic freedom.

A 1986 UN study done by Elizabeth Odio Benito, the Special Reporter of the UN commission on Human Rights, presented eight distinctive relationships between church and state:

1. State religions.
2. Established churches.
3. Neutral or secular states as regarding religion.
4. No official religion.
5. Separation of church from state.
6. Arrangements with the Roman Catholic Church.
7. Protection of legally recognized religious groups.
8. Millet system, recognizing a number of religious communities.

Elizabeth Odio Benito, *Study on the Current Dimensions of the Problems of Intolerance and Discrimination on Grounds of Religion or Belief*, (United Nations, Commission on Human Rights, 1986).

40    Dr. Benjamin Rush, (1745-1813) one of the youngest signers of the Declaration of Independence in 1776, was a distinguished physician and scientist who held the first chemistry professorship in America. He published the first American chemistry textbook, *A Syllabus of a Course of Lectures on Chemistry*, in 1770. He also established the first free dispensary in America in 1786 and published in 1812 the first American work on mental disorders, *Medical Inquiries and Observations Upon the Diseases of the Mind*. He helped to found the first abolition society in America, The Society for the Relief of Free Negroes Unlawfully Held in Bondage, in 1775, and was appointed by President John Adams as the Treasurer of the United States Mint in 1797, which he held until 1813. The following is taken from a personal letter written by Dr. Rush in the late 1700s: (Ck for 1st Vol. Of Am. Tract Soc. Pub of ATS-vol. 1, 1813)

"Dear Sir:

It is now several months since I promised to give you my reasons for preferring the Bible as a schoolbook to all other compositions. Before I state my arguments, I shall assume the five following propositions:

1. That Christianity is the only true and perfect religion; and that in proportion as mankind adopt its principles and obey its precepts they will be wise and happy.
2. That a better knowledge of this religion is to be acquired by reading the Bible than in any other way.
3. That the Bible contains more knowledge necessary to man in his present state than any other book in the world.
4. That knowledge is most durable, and religious instruction most useful, when imparted in early life.
5. That the Bible, when not read in schools, is seldom read in any subsequent period of life.

...I wish to be excused from repeating here that if the Bible did not convey a single direction for the attainment of future happiness, it should be read in our schools in preference to all other books from its containing the greatest portion of that kind of knowledge which is calculated to produce private and public temporal happiness.......I cannot but suspect that the present fashionable practice of rejecting the Bible from our schools has originated with Deists. And they discover great ingenuity in this new mode of attacking Christianity. If they proceed in it, they will do more in half a century in extirpating our religion than Bolingbroke or Voltaire could have effected in a thousand years.

But passing by all other considerations, and contemplating merely the political institutions of the United States, I lament that we waste so much time and money in punishing crimes and take so little pains to prevent them. We profess to be republicans, and yet we neglect the only means of establishing and perpetuating our republican forms of government; that is, the universal education of our youth in the principles of Christianity by means of the Bible; for this divine book, above all others, favors that equality among mankind, that respect for just laws, and all those sober and frugal virtues which constitute the soul of republicanism." (*The Bible in Schools*, Am. Tract Society)

41 George Washington's faith in Providence is seen following the Battle at the Monongahela in July, 1755, Washington wrote to his brother, John A. Washington on July 18, 1755:

"But by the all-powerful dispensations of Providence, I have been protected beyond all human probability or expectation; for I had four bullets through my coat, and two horses shot under me, yet escaped unhurt, although death was leveling my companions on every side of me." Consider also when Washington was addressed by an Indian chief in 1770. Traveling with Dr. Craik in Mononogahala area, Washington was addressed by an Indian chief through an interpreter:

"I am a chief and ruler over my tribes. My influence extends to the waters of the great lakes and to the far blue mountains.

I have traveled a long and weary path that I might see the young warrior of the great battle. It was on the day when the white man's blood mixed with the streams of our forests that I first beheld this chief [Washington]. I called to my young men and said, mark yon tall and daring warrior? He is not of the red-coat tribe—he hath an India's wisdom, and his warriors fight as we do—himself alone exposed.

Quick, let your aim be certain, and he dies. Our rifles were leveled, rifles which, but for you, knew not how to miss-'twas all in vain, a power mightier far than we, shielded you.

Seeing you were under the special guardianship of the Great Spirit, we immediately ceased to fire at you. I am old and soon shall be gathered to the great council fire of my fathers in the land of shades, but ere I go, there is something bids me speak in the voice of prophecy:

Listen! The Great Spirit protects that man [pointing at Washington], and guides his destinies—he will become the chief of nations, and a people yet unborn will hail him as the founder of a mighty empire. I am come to pay homage to the man who is the particular favorite of Heaven, and who can never die in battle." The famous Indian warrior, who was in that battle, said:

"Washington was never born to be killed by a bullet! I had seventeen fair fires at him with my rifle, and after all could not bring him down to the ground."

42 A summary of the evidence for George Washington's Christian faith is available from The Providence Forum.

43 A summary of our Presidents' views of the Bible is available from The Providence Forum.

44 William J. Federer, *America's God and Country*, 1994, 289

45 Alexis De Tocqueville was a French political scientist who toured America in 1831. His famous work *Democracy in America*, was first published in 1835 and 1840 and emphasized the intimate relationship between government, civil society and religion in the young republic.

46 "Brotherly Love" by John J. DiIulio Jr., *Wall Street Journal*, March 17, 2000, p. w13.

47 Coolidge, (John) Calvin. October 15, 1924, at the unveiling to the Equestrian Statue of Bishop Francis Asbury, Washington, D.C. *Calvin Coolidge, Foundations of the Republic Speeches and Addresses* (New York: Charles Scribner's Sons, 1926), pp. 149-155.

48 Consider the following cultural agenda statements that have been published: *The Homosexual Agenda*

Mike Swift said: "We shall sodomize your sons, emblems of your feeble masculinity, of your shallow dreams and vulgar lies. We shall seduce them in your schools, in your dormitories, in your gymnasiums, in your locker rooms, in your sports arenas, in your seminaries, in your youth groups, in your movie theater bathrooms, in your army bunkhouses, in your truck stops, in your all-male clubs, in your houses of Congress, wherever men are with men together. Your sons shall become our minions and do our bidding. They will be recast in our image. They will come to crave and adore us. ...

The family unit—spawning ground of lies, betrayals, mediocrity, hypocrisy and violence—will be abolished. The family unit, which only dampens imagination and curbs free will, must be eliminated. Perfect boys will be conceived and grown in the genetic laboratory. They will be bonded together in communal setting, under the control and instruction of homosexual savants.

All churches who condemn us will be closed. Our only gods are handsome young men. We adhere to a cult of beauty, morally esthetic. Al that is ugly and vulgar and banal will be annihilated. Since we are alienated from middle-class heterosexual conventions, we are free to live our lives according to the dictates of the pure imagination. For us too much is not enough. ...

All laws banning homosexual activity will be revoked. Instead, legislation shall be passed which engenders love between men. ...We shall rewrite history, history filled and debased with your heterosexual lies and distortions. We shall portray the homosexuality of the great leaders and thinkers who have shaped the world. We will demonstrate that homosexuality and intelligence and imagination are inextricably linked, and that homosexuality is a requirement for true nobility, true beauty in a man. ...

Tremble, hetero swine, when we appear before you without our masks." Quoted from "Homosexual Activist Outlines Goals of Homosexual Movement" By Mike Swift, "Gay Revolutionary" Reprinted from The Congressional Record. First printed in *Gay Community News*, February 15-21, 1987.

*The Islamic Agenda:*
A vision statement for the growth of Islam in America says,

"The Prophet established a city state and expanded it through da'wah, defensive wars and preemptive strikes against his enemies. The equivalent of that city state in America would be Islamic organizations and Muslim neighborhoods. We should promote Muslim neighborhoods in all major cites of the U.S. to serve as nuclei and expand them thought conversion and migration to the Muslim enclaves. The development of enclaves would give us control over the schools, local politics and help in establishing necessary institutional infrastructure. As these enclaves grow in size through conversion and immigration, the Muslims will have some say in national politics and perhaps even be able to elect Muslims as congressmen and senators. Naturally, at some point in time, we will be able to elect a Muslim as President in the White House. In time, we will be able to do what we cannot even say at this time. Defensive actions in our time, analogous to the defensive actions of the Prophet, would be to respond to the attackers on Islam in literature and the media. Preemptive strikes against the enemies of Islam, analogous to the preemptive strikes of the Prophet, would be ideological exposure of falsehood of secular humanism, secular nationalism, Christianity, Judaism, Hinduism, Buddhism and other religions and cults. However, in many cases mere presentation of the truth of Islam aggressively but rationally will be adequate to defeat the falsehood; Muslims may not need to attack other systems and religions."

(*Muslims and Christians at the Table*, Bruce McDowell and Anees Zaka, P&R Publishing, 1999, p. 145)
A survey of secular humanism and a survey of Communist thought as found in the writings of Karl Marx are available from The Providence Forum.

49     The Providence Forum has developed a letter: A Call for Christians to Vote. A copy may be obtained from The Providence Forum.

50     John Leo, *U.S. News & World Report*, 7/5/99.

51     Tryon Edwards, D.D., *The New Dictionary of Thought* (NY: Standard Book Company, 1955), p. 338.

52     Juliet Eilperin, *The Washington Post* and an Associated Press release in *The Washington Times*, 6/30/99. Rev. Barry W. Lynn is executive director of Americans United for Separation of Church and State.

53     "National Proclamation for a Day of Humiliation, Fasting, and Prayer." *A Compilation of the Messages and Papers of the Presidents*, 1:284-86. Gary DeMar, *Biblical World View*, (Atlanta, Georgia: An American Vision Publication, 1992), Vol. 8, no. 12, p. 9.

54     Robert Bork, *Slouching Towards Gomorrah* pages 5, 7, 337, 279.

55     Consider here J. Marcellus Kik, *Church & State: The Story of Two Kingdoms*, (New York: Thomas Nelson & Sons, 1963), pp. 118-21. "*The Liberal Movement within the Church*: The movement within the Church may be illustrated by a series of recommendations advocated by a Special Committee on Church and State, in a report given to the 1962 General Assembly of the United Presbyterian Church in the U. S. A. (See *Relations between Church and State, A Report to the 174ᵗʰ General Assembly*. Office of the General Assembly, Philadelphia, 1962.) The movement is by no means limited to the United Presbyterian Church, however—indeed, may be taken as

representative of an ever-increasing number of denominations.

The Report to the 174th General Assembly recommended, among other things, that there be a cessation of the celebration of religious holidays, Bible reading, and prayer in public schools; that Sabbath laws be made less stringent; that there be no tax exemptions for religious agencies; and that there be no special exemption from military service for ministerial candidates and ordained clergymen. The Report also questioned whether the clergy should serve as military chaplains paid by the State.

The above recommendations bear a remarkable resemblance to "the infidel program" to which Philip Schaff called attention in his excellent monograph, *Church and State in the United States*.

56    In the *Engel et al. v. Vitale et al.* case of 1962, the High Court said, "Because of the prohibition of the First Amendment against the enactment of any law 'respecting an establishment of religion,' which is made applicable to the States by the Fourteenth Amendment, state officials may not compose an official state prayer and require that it be recited in the public schools of the State at the beginning of each school day—even if the prayer is denominationally neutral and pupils who wish to do so may remain silent or be excused from the room while the prayer is being recited." 370 U. S., p. 42. In *School District of Abington, Pennsylvania, et al. v. Schempp* et al. the Supreme Court wrote in 1963, "Because of the prohibition of the First Amendment against the enactment by Congress of any law 'respecting an establishment of religion,' which is made applicable to the States by the Fourteenth Amendment, no state law or school board may require that passages from the Bible be read or that the Lord's Prayer be recited in the public schools of a State at the beginning of each school day—even if individual students may be excused from attending or participating in such exercises upon written request of their parents." 374 U. S. p. 203. See also the High Court's 1985 decision *in Wallace, Governor of Alabama, et al. v. Jaffree et al.*, 472 U. S. p. 39, "The State's endorsement, by enactment . . . of prayer activities at the beginning of each school day is not consistent with the established principle that the government must pursue a course of complete neutrality toward religion."

57    The *Roe v. Wade* decision said, "A state criminal abortion statute of the current Texas type, that excepts from criminality only a *life-saving* procedure on behalf of the mother, without regard to pregnancy stage and without recognition of the other interests involved, is violative of the Due Process Clause of the Fourteenth Amendment." 410 U.S. p. 164. Abortion is protected because "the Court has recognized that a right of personal privacy, or a guarantee of certain areas or zones of privacy, does exist under the Constitution." *Ibid.*, p. 152.

58    In the 1970 *Lemon et al. v. Kurtzman*, Superintendent of Public Instruction of Pennsylvania, et al. decision the High Court declared, "Under our system the choice has been made that government is to be entirely excluded from the area of religious instruction and churches excluded from the affairs of government. The Constitution decrees that religion must be a private matter for the individual, the family, and the institutions of private choice, and that while some involvement and entanglement are inevitable, lines must be drawn." The holding of the case creates a rigid secular vs. religious approach to legislation as seen in statements such as; ". . .with respect to children of impressionable age in the primary grades, and the dangers that a teacher under religious control and discipline poses to the separation of religious from purely secular aspects of elementary education in the schools;" ". . .ensure that teachers play a strictly non-ideological role and the state supervision of nonpublic school accounting procedures required to establish the cost of secular as distinguished from religious education." 403 U. S. p. 625, p. 603.

59    In the 1980 *Stone et al. v. Graham*, Superintendent of Public Instruction of Kentucky case, the High Court held, "A Kentucky statute requiring the posting of a copy of the Ten Commandments, purchased with private contributions, on the wall of each public school classroom in the State has no secular legislative purpose, and therefore is unconstitutional as violating the Establishment Clause of the First Amendment. While the state legislature required the notation in small print at the bottom of each that '[t]he secular application of the Ten Commandments is clearly seen in its adoption as the fundamental legal code of Western Civilization and the Common Law of the United States,' such an 'avowed' secular purpose is not sufficient to avoid conflict with the First Amendment. The pre-eminent purpose of posting the Ten Commandments, which do not confine themselves to arguably secular matters, is plainly religious in nature, and the posting serves no constitutional education function. *Cf. Abington School District v. Schempp*, 374 U. S. 203. That the posted copies are financed by voluntary private contributions is immaterial, for the mere posting under the auspices of the legislature

provides the official support of the state government that the Establishment Clause prohibits. Nor is it significant that the Ten Commandments are merely posted rather than read aloud, for it is no defense to urge that the religious practices may be relatively minor encroachments on the First Amendment ." 449 U. S., p. 39. In 1984, the Supreme Court made the following statement in *Lynch v. Donnelly*: "The Constitution [does not] require complete separation of church and state; it affirmatively mandates accommodation, not mere tolerance, of all religions, and forbids hostility toward any...Anything less would require the callous indifference we have said was never intended by the Establishment Clause...Indeed, we have observed such hostility would bring us into war with our national tradition as embodied in the First Amendment's guarantee of the free exercise of religion." In spite of this statement of "accommodation" of religion there continues to be a consistent effort to keep Christian influence from the public square.

60  The military's approach to the issue of homosexual soldiers, namely, "don't ask, don't tell" does not comport with American military history.  On March 10, 1778, in *Writings of George Washington*, 11:83-84, one reads, "At a General Court Marshall whereof Colo. Tupper was president (10th March 1778) Liett. Enslin of Colo. Malcom's Regiment tried for attempting to commit sodomy, with John Monhort a soldier; Secondly For Perjury in swearing to false Accounts, found guilty of the charges exhibited against him, being breaches of 5th Article 18th. Section of the Articles of War and do sentence him to be dismiss'd the service with Infamy.  His Excellency the Commander in Chief [George Washington] approves the sentence and with Abhorrence and Detestation of such Infamous Crimes orders Liett. Enslin to be drummed out of Camp tomorrow morning by all the Drummers and Fifers in the Army never to return; The Drummers and Fifers to attend on the Grand parade at Guard mounting for that Purpose."

61  Dr. Kevorkian has been the leading popularizer of euthanasia.  States across the country have various forms of legislation loosing historic standards against "mercy killing."

62  President Theodore Roosevelt clearly understood the impact of the High Court's removal of the Ten Commandments would have on public life.  In 1910 he said, "Every thinking man, when he thinks, realizes that the teachings of the Bible are so interwoven and entwined with our whole civic and social life that it would be literally impossible for us to figure ourselves what that life would be if these standards were removed.  We would lose almost all the standards by which we now judge both public and private morals; all the standards towards which we, with more or less resolution, strive to raise ourselves."

63  Brewer, David Josiah. 1905, *The United States - A Christian Nation* (Philadelphia, PA: The John C. Winston Company, 1905, Supreme Court Collection), pp. 11-12.

64  A. Hodge, professor of Systematic Theology at Princeton Seminary in the latter part of the nineteenth century made the case that the kingdom of God on earth is without borders, "but aims at absolute universality, and extends its supreme reign over every department of human life."  The implications of such a view are obvious: "It follows that it is the duty of every loyal subject to endeavor to bring all human society, social and political, as well as ecclesiastical, into obedience to its law of righteousness."  Hodge believed that there are comprehensive societal ramifications to the preaching and application of the Gospel.

It is our duty, as far as lies in our power, immediately to organize human society and all its intuitions and organs upon a distinctively Christian basis.  Indifference or impartiality here between the law of the kingdom and the law of the world, or of its prince, the devil, is utter treason to the King of Righteousness.  The Bible, the great statute-book of the kingdom, explicitly lays down principles which, when candidly applied, will regulate the action of every human being in all relations.  There can be no compromise. The King said, with regard to all descriptions of moral agents in all spheres of activity, "He that is not with me is against me."

If the national life in general is organized upon non-Christian principles, the churches which are embraced within the universal assimilating power of that nation will not long be able to preserve their integrity. Compromise is impossible.  Conflict is inevitable.  Neutrality is inconceivable.  Spiritual and ideological wars will continue whether Christians want to believe it or not.  The question is, are Christians prepared to fight?

65  Ibid., Vol. 30, 5-5-1789. To James Madison, "As the first of every thing, *in our situation* will serve to establish a Precedent, it is devoutly wished on my part, that these precedent may be fixed on true principles."

66   Willard Sterne Randall, *George Washington A Life* (New York: Henry Holt and Company, 1997) p. 256. He writes: "Washington was not a deeply religious man."

67   Douglas Southall Freeman, *George Washington, A Biography Victory with the Help of France* (New York: Charles Scribner's Sons, 1952), Vol. 5, p. 493.

68   James Thomas Flexner, *The Indispensable Man*, p. 216.

69   *WGW* Vol. 30, 10-3-1789.

70   Ibid., Vol. 12-17-1778.

71   Ibid., Vol. 5, 5-31-1776.

72   Ibid., Vol. 30, 4-1789.

73   Ibid., Vol. 2-7-1788. To Marquis de Lafayette. "You appear to be, as might be expected from a real friend to this Country, anxiously concerned about its present political situation. So far as I am able I shall be happy in gratifying that friendly solicitude. As to my sentiments with respect to the merits of the new Constitution, I will disclose them without reserve, (although by passing through the Post offices they should become known to all the world) for, in truth, I have nothing to conceal on that subject. It appears to me, then, little short of a miracle, that the Delegates from so many different States (which States you know are also different from each other in their manners, circumstances and prejudices) should unite in forming a system of national Government, so little liable to well founded objections. Nor am I yet such an enthusiastic, partial or undiscriminating admirer of it, as not to perceive it is tinctured with some real (though not radical) defects. The limits of a letter would not suffer me to go fully into an examination of them; nor would the discussion be entertaining or profitable, I therefore forbear to touch upon it. With regard to the two great points (the pivots upon which the whole machine must move,) my Creed is simply,

1st. That the general Government is not invested with more Powers than are indispensably necessary to perform the functions of a good Government; and, consequently, that no objection ought to be made against the quantity of Power delegated to it.

2ly. That these Powers (as the appointment of all Rulers will for ever arise from, and, at short stated intervals, recur to the free suffrage of the People) are so distributed among the Legislative, Executive, and Judicial Branches, into which the general Government is arranged, that it can never be in danger of degenerating into a monarchy, an Oligarchy, an Aristocracy, or any other despotic or oppressive form, so long as there shall remain any virtue in the body of the People.

I would not be understood my dear Marquis to speak of consequences which may be produced, in the revolution of ages, by corruption of morals, profligacy of manners, and listlessness for the preservation of the natural and unalienable rights of mankind; nor of the successful usurpations that may be established at such an unpropitious juncture, upon the ruins of liberty, however providently guarded and secured, as these are contingencies against which no human prudence can effectually provide. It will at least be a recommendation to the proposed Constitution that it is provided with more checks and barriers against the introduction of Tyranny, and those of a nature less liable to be surmounted, than any Government hitherto instituted among mortals, hath possessed. We are not to expect perfection in this world; but mankind, in modern times, have apparently made some progress in the science of government. Should that which is now offered to the People of America, be found on experiment less perfect than it can be made, a Constitutional door is left open for its amelioration."

74   Ibid., Vol. 29, 11-10-1787. To Bushrod Washington. "The warmest friends and the best supporters the Constitution has, do not contend that it is free from imperfections; but they found them unavoidable and are sensible, if evil is likely to arise there from, the remedy must come hereafter; for in the present moment, it is not to be obtained; and, as there is a Constitutional door open for it, I think the People (for it is with them to Judge) can as they will have the advantage of experience on their Side, decide with as much propriety on the alterations and amendments which are necessary [as] ourselves. I do not think we are more inspired, have more wisdom, or possess more virtue, than those who will come after us.

The power under the Constitution will always be in the People. It is entrusted for certain defined purposes, and for a certain limited period, to representatives of their own chusing; and whenever it is executed contrary to their Interest, or not agreeable to their wishes, their Servants can, and undoubtedly will be, recalled. It is agreed on all hands that no government can be well administered without powers; . . . No man is a warmer advocate for proper restraints and wholesome checks in every department of government than I am; but I have never yet been able to discover the propriety of placing it absolutely out of the power of men to render essential Services, because a possibility remains of their doing ill."

75 *Records of the Federal Convention*, Saturday, June 30, Yates: Mr. Bedford: "That all the states at present are equally sovereign and independent, has been asserted from every quarter of this house. Our deliberations here are a confirmation of the position; and I may add to it, that each of them act from interested, and many from ambitious motives. Look at the votes which have been given on the floor of this house, and it will be found that their numbers, wealth and local views, have actuated their determination; and that the larger states proceed as if our eyes were already perfectly blinded. Impartiality, with them, is already out of the question — the reported plan is their political creed, and they support it, right or wrong....Pretenses to support ambition are never wanting. Their cry is, where is the danger? And they insist that altho' the powers of the general government will be increased, yet it will be for the good of the whole; and although the three great states form nearly a majority of the people of America, they never will hurt or injure the lesser states. I do not, gentleman trust you. If you possess the power, the abuse of it could not be checked; and what then would prevent you from exercising it to our destruction?"

*Elliot's The Debates in the Several State Conventions on the Adoption of the Federal Constitution Vol. 1 image 500 or 606.*

*http://memory.loc.gov/cgibin/ampage?collId=llfr&fileName=001/llfr001.db&recNum=529&itemLink =r?ammem/hlaw:@field(DOCID+@lit(fr001145))%230010510&linkText=1*

Friday, June 17, Section 8, was again read, and

"The Hon. Mr. SMITH rose. Perhaps there never was a government which, in the course of ten years, did not do something to be repented of. As for Rhode Island, I do not mean to justify her; she deserves to be condemned. If there were in the world but one example of political depravity, it would be hers; and no nation ever merited, or suffered, a more genuine infamy than a wicked administration has attached to her character. Massachusetts also has been guilty of errors, and has lately been distracted by an internal convulsion. Great Britain, notwithstanding her boasted constitution, has been a perpetual scene of revolutions and civil war. Her Parliaments have been abolished; her kings have been banished and murdered. I assert that the majority of the governments in the Union have operated better than any body had reason to expect, and that nothing but experience and habit is wanting to give the state laws all the stability and wisdom necessary to make them respectable, if these things be true, I think we ought not to exchange our condition, with a hazard of losing our state constitutions. We all agree that a general government is necessary; but it ought not to go so far as to destroy the authority of the members. We shall be unwise to make a new experiment, in so important a matter, without some known and sure grounds to go upon. The state constitutions should be the guardians of our domestic rights and interests, and should be both the support and the check of the federal government." Ibid., Vol. 2, image 335 of 556.

*Records of the Federal Convention*, Saturday, July 11.

"Mr. <Madison> was not a little surprised to hear this implicit confidence urged by a member who on all occasions, had inculcated so strongly, the political depravity of men, and the necessity of checking one vice and interest by opposing to them another vice & interest." Ibid. Vol. 5, image 298 of 641.

76 *WGW* Vol. 29, 4-28-1788. To Lafayette, "This I lay out to be a letter of Politics. ...at present, or under our existing form of Confederations, it would be idle to think of making commercial regulations on our part. One State passes a prohibitory law respecting some article, another State opens wide the avenue for its admission. One Assembly makes a system, another Assembly unmakes it. Virginia, in the very last session of her Legislature, was about to have passed some of the most extravagant and preposterous Edicts on the subject of trade that ever stained the leaves of a Legislative Code. It is in vain to hope for a remedy of these and innumerable other evils, untill a general Government shall be adopted.

The Conventions of Six States only have as yet accepted the new Constitution. No one has rejected it. It is believed that the Convention of Maryland, which is now in session; and that of South Carolina, which is to assemble on the 12th of May, will certainly adopt it. It is, also, since the elections of Members for the Convention have taken place in this State, more generally believed that it will be adopted here than it was before those elections were made. There will, however, be powerful and eloquent speeches on both sides of the question in the Virginia Convention; but as Pendleton, Wythe, Blair, Madison, Jones, Nicholas, Innis and many other of our first characters will be advocates for its adoption, you may suppose the weight of abilities will rest on that side. Henry and Mason are its great adversaries. The Governor, if he opposes it at all will do it feebly.

On the general merits of this proposed Constitution, I wrote to you, some time ago, my sentiments pretty freely. That letter had not been received by you, when you addressed to me the last of yours which has come to my hands. I had never supposed that perfection could be the result of accommodation and mutual concession. The opinion of Mr. Jefferson and yourself is certainly a wise one, that the Constitution ought by all means to be accepted by nine States before any attempt should be made to procure amendments. For, if that acceptance shall not previously take place, men's minds will be so much agitated and soured, that the danger will be greater than ever of our becoming a disunited People. Whereas, on the other hand, with prudence in temper and a spirit of moderation, every essential alteration, may in the process of time, be expected.

You will doubtless, have seen, that it was owing to this conciliatory and patriotic principle that the Convention of Massachusetts adopted the Constitution in toto; but recommended a number of specific alterations and quieting explanations, as an early, serious and unremitting subject of attention. Now, although it is not to be expected that every individual, in Society, will or can ever be brought to agree upon what is, exactly, the best form of government; yet, there are many things in the Constitution which only need to be explained, in order to prove equally satisfactory to all parties. For example: there was not a member of the convention, I believe, who had the least objection to what is contended for by the Advocates for a *Bill of Rights* and *Tryal by Jury* . The first, where the people evidently retained every thing which they did not in express terms give up, was considered nugatory as you will find to have been more fully explained by Mr. Wilson and others: And as to the second, it was only the difficulty of establishing a mode which should not interfere with the fixed modes of any of the States, that induced the Convention to leave it, as a matter of future adjustment.

There are other points on which opinions would be more likely to vary. As for instance, on the ineligibility of the same person for President, after he should have served a certain course of years. Guarded so effectually as the proposed Constitution is, in respect to the prevention of bribery and undue influence in the choice of President: I confess, I differ widely myself from Mr. Jefferson and you, as to the necessity or expediency of rotation in that appointment. The matter was fairly discussed in the Convention, and to my full convictions; though I cannot have time or room to sum up the argument in this letter. There cannot, in my judgment, be the least danger that the President will by any practicable intrigue ever be able to continue himself one moment in office, much less perpetuate himself in it; but in the last stage of corrupted morals and political depravity: and even then there is as much danger that any other species of domination would prevail. Though, when a people shall have become incapable of governing themselves and fit for a master, it is of little consequence from what quarter he comes. Under an extended view of this part of the subject, I can see no propriety in precluding ourselves from the services of any man, who on some great emergency shall be deemed universally, most capable of serving the Public."

77    Ibid., Vol. 30, 4-1789. Proposed Address to Congress: "set up my judgment as the standard of perfection? And shall I arrogantly pronounce that whosoever differs from me, must discern the subject through a distorting medium, or be influenced by some nefarious design? The mind is so formed in different persons as to contemplate the same object in different points of view. Hence originates the difference on questions of the greatest import, both human and divine. In all Institutions of the former kind, great allowances are doubtless to be made for the fallibility and imperfection of their authors. Although the agency I had informing this system, and the high opinion I entertained of my Colleagues for their ability and integrity may have tended to warp my judgment in its favour; yet I will not pretend to say that it appears absolutely perfect to me, or that there may not be many faults which have escaped my discernment. ....Whether the Constitutional door that is opened for amendments in ours, be not the wisest and apparently the happiest expedient that has ever been suggested by human prudence I leave to every unprejudiced mind to determine. Under these circumstances I conclude it has been the part of wisdom to ad[vise] it. I pretend to no unusual foresight into futurity, and therefore cannot undertake to decide, with certainty, what may be its ultimate fate. If a promised good should terminate in an unexpected evil, it would not be a solitary example of disappointment in this mutable state of

existence. If the blessings of Heaven showered thick around us should be spilled on the ground or converted to curses, through the fault of those for whom they were intended, it would not be the first instance of folly or perverseness in short-sighted mortals. The blessed Religion revealed in the word of God will remain an eternal and awful monument to prove that the best Institutions may be abused by human depravity; and that they may even, in some instances be made subservient to the vilest of purposes. Should, hereafter, those who are intrusted with the management of this government, incited by the lust of power and prompted by the Supineness or venality of their Constituents, overleap the known barriers of this Constitution and violate the unalienable rights of humanity: it will only serve to shew, that no compact among men (however provident in its construction and sacred in its ratification) can be pronounced everlasting and inviolable, and if I may so express myself, that no Wall of words, that no mound of parchmt. can be so formed as to stand against the sweeping torrent of boundless ambition on the one side, aided by the sapping current of corrupted morals on the other."

78    In the New England mind of the day, civil and religious liberty were inseparable, and thus the happiness of life required a full liberty to pursue both. The Declaration of Independence spoke of "inalienable rights" with which Americans had been endowed by "our Creator" which included "life, liberty and the pursuit of happiness." The word "happiness" in the American context included implications for eternal salvation. (See, for example, Noah Webster's *magnum opus, An American Dictionary of the English Language*, published in 1834, wherein his definitions of "happy" and "happiness" encompassed the blessedness of the afterlife in Heaven.) America's spiritual happiness was intimately connected with her political happiness, as seen in the words of the political triumvirate of the New England Adams dynasty: See endnote 4 and pages 40 and 46 of the text.

79    This powerful and illuminating letter in terms of the Christian perspective of Washington's religion is here quoted in full. *The Papers of George Washington*, W. W. Abbot, Ed., Dorothy Twohig, Assoc. Ed., *Presidential Series* (Charlottesville: University Press of Virginia), Vol. 6, pp. 279-282. This will be abbreviated by *PGW*, volume number, page number *PGW* Vol. 4:275-277:

"And now we devoutly offer our humble tribute of praise and thanksgiving to the all-gracious *Father* of *lights* who has inspired our public Councils with a wisdom and firmness, which have effected that desirable purpose, in so great a measure by the National-Constitution, and who has fixed the eyes of all America on you as the worthiest of its Citizens to be entrusted with the execution of it.

Whatever any may have supposed wanting in the original plan, we are happy to find so wisely providing in it amendments; and it is with peculiar satisfaction we behold how easily the entire confidence of the People, in the Man who sits at the helm of Government, has eradicated every remaining objection to its form.

Among these we never considered the want of *a religious test*, that grand engine of persecution in every tyrant's hand: but we should not have been alone in rejoicing to have seen some Explicit acknowledgement of the *only true God and Jesus Christ, whom he hath sent* inserted some where in the *Magna Charta* of our country.

We are happy to find, however, that this defect has been amply remedied, in the face of all the world, by the piety and devotion, in which your first public act of office was performed—by the religious observance of the Sabbath, and of the public worship of *God*, of which you have set so eminent an example—and by the warm strains of Christian and devout affections, which run through your late proclamation, for a general thanksgiving. The catholic spirit breathed in all your public acts supports us in the pleasing assurance that no religious establishments—no exclusive privileges tending to elevate one denomination of Christians to the depression of the rest shall ever be ratified by the signature of the *President* during your administration

On the contrary we bless God that your whole deportment bids all denominations confidently to expect to find in you the watchful guardian of their equal liberties—the steady patron of genuine Christianity—and the bright Exemplar of those peculiar virtues, in which its distinguishing doctrines have their proper effect.

Under the nurturing hand of a Ruler of such virtues, and one so deservedly revered by all ranks, we joyfully indulge the hope that virtue and religion will revive and flourish—that infidelity and the vices ever attendant in its train, will be banished [from] every polite circle; and that rational piety will soon become fashionable there; and from thence be diffused among all other ranks in the community.

Captivated with the delightful prospect of a national reformation rising out of the influence of your authority and example; we find the fullest encouragement to cherish the hope of it, from the signal deeds of pious and patriotic heroism, which marked the steps of the Father of his country, from the memorable hour of his appearance in Congress, to declare the disinterested views with which he accepted the command of her armies, to that hour, not less memorable, when, having gloriously acquitted himself in that important trust, and completely accomplished the design of it, he appeared in the same great Assembly again; and resigned his commission into the hands that gave it.

But glorious as your course has been as a Soldier in arms, defending your country, and the rights of mankind; we exult in the presage that it will be far outshone by the superior luster of a more glorious career now before you, as the Chief Magistrate of your nation—protecting, by just and merciful laws—and by a wise, firm, and temperate execution of them, enhancing the value of those inestimable rights and privileges, which you have so worthily asserted to it by your sword.

Permit us then, great Sir, to assure you that whilst it ever shall be our care, in our several places to inculcate those principles, drawn from the pure fountains of light and truth, in the sacred scriptures, which can best recommend your virtues to their imitation, and which, if generally obeyed, would contribute essentially to render your people happy, and your government prosperous; Our unceasing prayers to the *great Sovereign of all* nations, shall be that your important life, and all your singular talents may be the special care of an indulgent Providence for many years to come; that your administration may be continued to your country, under the peculiar smiles of Heaven, long be continued to your country, under the peculiar smiles of Heaven, long enough to advance the interests of learning to the zenith—to carry the arts and sciences to their destined perfection—to chase ignorance, bigotry, and immorality off the stage—to restore true virtue, and the religion of *Jesus* to their deserved throne in our land: and to found the liberties of America, both religious and civil, on a basis which no era of futurity shall ever see removed: and, finally, that, when you have thus done—free grace may confer on you, as the reward of all your great labours, the unfading laurels of an everlasting crown." Joseph Prince, moderator on behalf of the First Presbytery

80   *Westminster Confession of Faith*, chapter I, paragraph vii, "All things in Scripture are not alike plain in themselves, nor alike clear unto all; yet those things which are necessary to be known, believed, and observed, for salvation, are so clearly propounded and opened in some place of Scripture or other, that not only the learned, but the unlearned, in a due use of the ordinary means, may attain unto a sufficient understanding of them." In Schaff, *Creeds of Christendom*, Vol. III, p. 604.

81   *WGW* Vol. 30, 10-23-1789, note.

82   Rev. Dr. John Witherspoon was a Presbyterian Minister from New Jersey, President of the College of New Jersey in Princeton, and a member of Congress. He was the only clergyman to sign the Declaration of Independence. In 1782, he composed one of the Continental Congress' national calls for a day of thanksgiving: ". . . to testify their gratitude to God for his goodness, by a cheerful obedience to his laws, and by promoting, each in his station, and by his influence, the practice of true and undefiled religion, which is the great foundation of public prosperity and national happiness." Note that in his mind as an orthodox minister in the Presbyterian tradition, "true and undefiled religion" was a synonym for Christianity. Witherspoon did not directly mention the name of Jesus Christ in his proclamation, but this obviously had no anti-Christian or deistic intent. See *Journals of the Continental Congress*, on the date specified.

83   *PGW*, 2:424. As Washington said at the conclusion of his letter to the Virginia Baptists, "In the meantime be assured, Gentlemen, that I entertain a proper sense of your fervent supplications to God for my temporal and eternal happiness."

84   We will consider Washington's belief in heaven and eternal life in a latter chapter. For now, notice that he understands happiness as both temporal and future in the hereafter. The import of the "completion" of happiness is eternity. *WGW* Vol. 25, 11-16-1782. To the Reformed Protestant Dutch Church in Kingston. "In return for your kind concern for my temporal and eternal happiness, permit me to assure you that my wishes are reciprocal...." Ibid., Vol. 6, 11-4-1798.to Rev. William Lynn, who had been Chaplain to Congress under Washington's Presidency and was a Reformed minister from New York City. "Revd. Sir: I received with thankfulness your favour of the 30th. Ulto., enclosing the discourse delivered by you on the day recommended by the President of the United States to be observed as a general Fast. I have read them both with pleasure; and feel grateful for the favourable sentiments you have been pleased to express in my behalf; but more especially for those good wishes which you offer for my temporal and eternal happiness; which I reciprocate with great

cordiality…."

85    Ibid., Vol. 30, 4-30-1789. …..it would be peculiarly improper to omit, in this first official act, my fervent supplications to that Almighty Being who rules over the universe, who presides in the councils of nations and whose providential aids can supply every human defect; that His benediction may consecrate to the liberties and happiness of the people of the United States a Government instituted by themselves for these essential purposes; and may enable every instrument employed in its administration to execute with success, the functions allotted to his charge.

In tendering this homage to the Great Author of every public and private good, I assure myself that it expresses your sentiments not less than my own….

86    Ibid., Vol. 30, 4-30-1789, "No People can be bound to acknowledge and adore the invisible hand, which conducts the Affairs of men more than the People of the United States. Every step, by which they have advanced to the character of an independent nation, seems to have been distinguished by some token of providential agency. And in the important revolution just accomplished in the system of their United Government, the tranquil deliberations and voluntary consent of so many distinct communities, from which the event has resulted, cannot be compared with the means by which most Governments have been established, without some return of pious gratitude along with an humble anticipation of the future blessings which the past seem to presage. These reflections, arising out of the present crisis, have forced themselves too strongly on my mind to be suppressed. You will join with me I trust in thinking, that there are none under the influence of which, the proceedings of a new and free Government can more auspiciously commence."

87    Ibid., Vol. 30, 4-30-1789, "And in the important revolution just accomplished, in the system of their United government, the tranquil deliberations and voluntary consent of so many distinct communities, from which the event has resulted, can not be compared with the means by which most governments have been established, without some return of pious gratitude, along with an humble anticipation of the future blessings which the past seem to presage."

88    Ibid., Vol. 30, 4-30-1789, "We ought to be no less persuaded that the propitious smiles of Heaven can never be expected on a nation that disregards the eternal rules of order and right which Heaven itself has ordained; and since the preservation of the sacred fire of liberty and the destiny of the republican model of government are justly considered as deeply, perhaps finally, staked on the experiment."

89    Lillback, *Proclaim Liberty*, p. 84-86; Sanford H. Cobb, *The Rise of Religious Liberty in America* (New York: Macmillan Co., 1902), p. 419.

90    This was, of course, in New York City. The U.S. Capitol wasn't moved to Washington, D.C., until several years later. After the World Trade Center was destroyed on September 11, 2001, by Muslim extremists, Mayor Guiliani marveled to the world how St. Paul's Cathedral, within the shadow of these towering giants, miraculously survived their destruction.

91    *Soldier and Servant Series: Mrs. Alexander Hamilton Witness that George Washington Was A Communicant of the Church* (Hartford: Church Missions Publishing Company, 1932).

92    *PGW*, 6:279-282.

93    Ibid., 5:299-301.

94    Ibid., 3:496-499.

95    Ibid., 2:179-181; *PGW*, 8:181-82.

96    Ibid., 3:92-93.

97    Ibid., 4:263-265.

98    Ibid., 2:420-422; *PGW*, 4:274-277.

99    Ibid., 4:198-199; *PGW*, 8:177-178.

100   Ibid., 3:466-467; *PGW*, 8:226-227.

101   Ibid., 2:411-412.

102   Ibid., 2:423-425.

103   Ibid., 4:265-269; *PGW*, 5:296-299.

104   Ibid., 6:287-288; *PGW*, 4:182-183.

105   Ibid., 6:223-225.

106 Ibid., 5:448-450; *PGW*, 6:284-286; *PGW*, 7:61-64.

107 Ibid., 12:40-41.

108 Ibid., 2:179-181.

109 Ibid., 2:411-412.

110 Ibid., 3:92.

111 See notes 2, 3, 4 above.

112 *WGW* Vol. 27, 6-11-1783. Responding to Rev. Rodgers proposal for Congress to present each soldier with a Bible, Washington wrote, "Dear Sir: I accept, with much pleasure your kind Congratulations on the happy Event of Peace, with the Establishment of our Liberties and Independence. Glorious indeed has been our Contest: glorious, if we consider the Prize for which we have contended, and glorious in its Issue; but in the midst of our Joys, I hope we shall not forget that, to divine Providence is to be ascribed the Glory and the Praise. Your proposition respecting Mr. Aikins Bible would have been particularly noticed by me, had it been suggested in Season; but the late Resolution of Congress for discharging Part of the Army, takg off near two thirds of our Numbers, it is now too late to make the Attempt. It would have pleased me, if Congress should have made such an important present, to the brave fellows, who have done so much for the Security of their Country's Rights and Establishment."

113 *PGW*, 2:420-422.

114 Ibid., 2:420-421.

115 Ibid., 2:420-422, "While all men within our territories are protected in worshipping the Deity according to the dictates of their consciences; it is rationally to be expected from them in return. . . ."

116 Ibid. Vol. 12, 8-20-1778 to Gen. Thomas Nelson; Ibid. Vol. 28, 9-5-1785, to Chevelier de Luzerne.

117 James Madison, Virginia Convention, June 6, 1788. In Padover, *The Complete Madison*, p. 339.

118 Abraham Lincoln, *Great Speeches* (Mineola, N. Y.: Dover, 1991), p. 2.

\* For sources not cited in the text, please contact The Providence Forum for a complete list.

## ILLUSTRATION CREDITS

Dwight D. Eisenhower, No known restrictions on publication. Courtesy of the Prints and Photographs Division. Library of Congress. Reproduction Number: LC-USZ62-117123

Lincoln's address at the dedication of the Gettysburg National Cemetery, November 19, 1863 No known restrictions on publication. Courtesy of the Prints and Photographs Division. Library of Congress. Reproduction Number: LC-USZ62-2006

Theodore Roosevelt No known restrictions on publication. Courtesy of the Prints and Photographs Division. Library of Congress. Reproduction Number: LC-USZ62-13026

Samuel Adams No known restrictions on publication. Courtesy of the Prints and Photographs Division. Library of Congress. Reproduction Number: LC-USZ62-102271

John Hancock No known restrictions on publication. Courtesy of the Prints and Photographs Division. Library of Congress. Reproduction Number: LC-USZ62-29410

Benjamin Franklin No known restrictions on publication. Courtesy of the Prints and Photographs Division. Library of Congress. Reproduction Number: LC-USZ62-25564

John Quincy Adams No known restrictions on publication. Courtesy of the Prints and Photographs Division. Library of Congress. Reproduction Number: LC-USZ62-117119

Woodrow Wilson No known restrictions on publication. Courtesy of the Prints and Photographs Division. Library of Congress. Reproduction Number: LC-USZ62-13028

Ronald Reagan No known restrictions on publication. Courtesy of the Prints and Photographs Division. Library of Congress. Reproduction Number: LC-USZ62-13040

The Ten Commandments plaque at the Chester County Courthouse. Photo by David Williams, County of Chester, Pennsylvania.

George Washington No known restrictions on publication. Courtesy of the Prints and Photographs Division. Library of Congress. Reproduction Number: LC-USZ62-105109

Gouverneur Morris No known restrictions on publication. Courtesy of the Prints and Photographs Division. Library of Congress. Reproduction Number: LC-USZ62-45482

Benjamin Rush No known restrictions on publication. Courtesy of the Prints and Photographs Division. Library of Congress. Reproduction Number: LC-USZ62-54697

James Madison No known restrictions on publication. Courtesy of the Prints and Photographs Division. Library of Congress. Reproduction Number: LC-USZ62-13004

Harry S. Truman No known restrictions on publication. Courtesy of the Prints and Photographs Division. Library of Congress. Reproduction Number: LC-USZ62-117122

William O. Douglas No known restrictions on publication. Courtesy of the Prints and Photographs Division. Library of Congress. Reproduction Number: LC-USZ62-44543

US Supreme Court Chief Justice William H. Rehnquist No known restrictions on publication. Courtesy of the Prints and Photographs Division. Library of Congress. Reproduction Number: LC-USZC6-28

Depictions of the Ten Commandments in the US Supreme Court Building – These images are works of an employee of the Supreme Court of the United States, taken or made during the course of the person's official duties. As works of the U.S. federal government, the images are in the public domain.

Thomas Jefferson No known restrictions on publication. Courtesy of the Prints and Photographs Division. Library of Congress. Reproduction Number: LC-USZ62-117117

George W. Bush - © Brooks Kraft/Corbis

The Islamic Society of Northern Wisconsin – image in the public domain, courtesy of Wikimedia Commons.

The Providence Forum's Spirit of Liberty Bell – photo courtesy of Ralf W. Augstroze (www.ProvidenceForum.org)

Ground Zero - This image is a work of a sailor or employee of the U.S. Navy, taken or made during the course of the person's official duties. As a work of the U.S. federal government, the image is in the public domain.

Karl Marx – No known restrictions on publication. Courtesy of the Prints and Photographs Division. Library of Congress. REPRODUCTION NUMBER: LC-USZ62-16530

Christopher Columbus - No known restrictions on publication. Courtesy of the Prints and Photographs Division.

Library of Congress. Reproduction Number: LC-USZC2-1687

The signing of the Mayflower Compact - No known restrictions on publication. Courtesy of the Prints and Photographs Division. Library of Congress. Reproduction Number: LC-DIG-ppmsca-07842

Andrew Jackson - No known restrictions on publication. Courtesy of the Prints and Photographs Division. Library of Congress. Reproduction Number: LC-USZ62-117120

Calvin Coolidge - No known restrictions on publication. Courtesy of the Prints and Photographs Division. Library of Congress. Reproduction Number: LC-USZ62-13030

Martin Luther King - This file has been released into the public domain by its author, U.S. News & World Report Magazine (Collection at the U.S. Library of Congress). U.S. News & World Report Magazine (Collection at the U.S. Library of Congress) grants anyone the right to use this work for any purpose, without any conditions, unless such conditions are required by law.

Omar N. Bradley - No known restrictions on publication. Courtesy of the Prints and Photographs Division. Library of Congress. Reproduction Number: LC-USZ62-34071

David Josiah Brewer - No known restrictions on publication. Courtesy of the Prints and Photographs Division. Library of Congress. Reproduction Number: LC-USZ62-83098

The Constitution of the United States - This image is a work of an employee of the National Archives and Records Administration of the United States, taken or made during the course of the person's official duties. As a work of the U.S. federal government, the image is in the public domain.

J. Gresham Machen – used with the permission of the Archives of Montgomery Library at Westminister Theological Seminary, Philadelphia, PA.

Francis Schaeffer – image courtesy of Crossway Books

The Prayer at Valley Forge - No known restrictions on publication. Courtesy of the Prints and Photographs Division. Library of Congress. Reproduction Number: LC-DIG-pga-02160

Independence Hall - This work is in the public domain in the United States because it is a work of the United States Federal Government under the terms of Title 17, Chapter 1, Section 105 of the US Code.

The Marquis de Lafayette - No known restrictions on publication. Courtesy of the Prints and Photographs Division. Library of Congress. Reproduction Number: LC-USZC4-676

The first prayer in congress - No known restrictions on publication. Courtesy of the Prints and Photographs Division. Library of Congress. Reproduction Number: LC-DIG-pga-03229

John F. Kennedy - No known restrictions on publication. Courtesy of the Prints and Photographs Division. Library of Congress. Reproduction Number: LC-USZ62-117124

Abraham Lincoln - No known restrictions on publication. Courtesy of the Prints and Photographs Division. Library of Congress. Reproduction Number: LC-USZ62-13016

# THE PROVIDENCE FORUM

...proclaiming liberty throughout the land

The doctrine of Providence declares that the world and our lives are not ruled by chance or by fate, but by God. The Providence Forum demonstrably acknowledges that the Providence of God continues to be at work, and calls us to action. It is a non-profit corporation whose mission is to reinstill and promote a Judeo-Christian worldview within our culture and to advance the faith, ethics, and moral values consistent with the spirit of our nation's founding, emphasizing America's historical Judeo-Christian roots. The Providence Forum reaches a broad, national audience using various means, including multimedia, radio, television and film, publications, conferences, and lectures among its many channels of communication. The Providence Forum has been raised up to help call our nation back to its historic dependence on what both George Washington and Thomas Jefferson called "an overruling Providence." Our founding father, George Washington, spoke of, "That overruling Providence which has so often, and so remarkably interposed in our favor." He wrote, "you will permit me to remind you, as an inexhaustible subject of consolation, that there is a good Providence which will never fail to take care of his Children."

www.ProvidenceForum.org

# PROVIDENCE
# FORUM PRESS

Providence Forum Press is the publishing arm of The Providence Forum. Its mission is to present the facts and opinions of scholarly and mainstream authors on topics relating to the Judeo-Christian heritage of the United States and divine Providence in America and around the world.

The "all-seeing eye of Providence" is a symbol that has needlessly been shrouded in mystery and controversy throughout US history, in spite of its clear message and meaning. It is found on the Great Seal of the United States, which was conceived by various committees of the US Congress beginning in 1776, but the final form we see today was proposed in the summer of 1782 by Secretary of Congress Charles Thomson, a Christian theologian. His design of the Great Seal of the United States displayed the "eye of Providence," encased in a triangle representing the Trinity, signifying the historic Christian icon of God the Father, the first person of the Trinity, the Sovereign Agent of Providence. According to the records of the Continental Congress, " . . . the eye . . . allude[s] to the many signal interpositions of providence in favour of the American cause." Other organizations subsequently adopted similar symbolism as early as 1797 for purposes other than this original intent. Even The Masonic Service Association of North America confirms, "The eye on the [Great] Seal represents an active intervention of God in the affairs of men," and, "When placed in a triangle, the eye went beyond a general representation of God to a strongly Trinitarian statement." It goes on to conclude, referring to the back of the Great Seal, "The combining of the eye of Providence overlooking an unfinished pyramid is a uniquely American—not Masonic—icon, and must be interpreted as its designers intended. It has no Masonic context." (Masonic Service Association of North America, "Eye in the Pyramid" at http://www.msana.com/eyeinpyramid.asp)

This historic image is both an American and Christian symbol of our founding fathers, and, is thus most appropriate as the publisher's mark of Providence Forum Press.

# About the Author

 Peter A. Lillback, Ph.D., is the president of The Providence Forum, senior pastor at Proclamation Presbyterian Church in Bryn Mawr, Pennsylvania, and president of Westminster Theological Seminary, where he is also Professor of Historical Theology. He is the voice of *Proclaiming The Word*, a daily syndicated radio program, as well as *The Proclamation Worship Hour*. Dr. Lillback received a Ph.D. from Westminster Theological Seminary, a Th.M. from Dallas Theological Seminary, and a B.A. from Cedarville University in Ohio. He is the author of the bestselling epic book *George Washington's Sacred Fire* (Providence Forum Press), *The Binding of God: Calvin's Role in the Development of Covenant Theology* (Baker), *Freedom's Holy Light—With a Firm Reliance on Divine Providence* (Providence Forum Press), and *Proclaim Liberty: A Broken Bell Rings Freedom to the World* (Providence Forum Press).

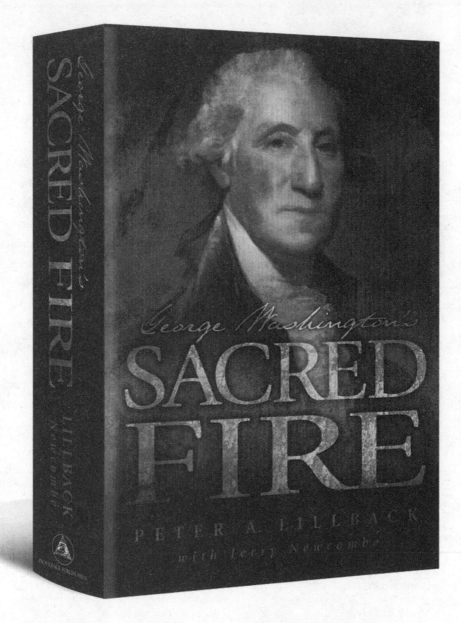

George Washington's
SACRED FIRE

PETER A. LILLBACK
with Jerry Newcombe

Available from better bookstores, or from
www.ProvidenceForum.org, (866) 55-FORUM (toll free)

*"...perhaps the finest book available on the nation's first president..."*

WorldNetDaily

*"...Dr. Lillback buries the myth that Washington was an unbeliever —
at most a "deist" -under an avalanche of facts..."*

Robert P. George, Princeton University

*"...It critiques and debunks the evidence used by 20th century scholars to
'prove' that Washington was a Deist...it has stirred-up the status-quo
historical community across the nation...The book builds a compelling
case...Lillback's evidence strongly supports his premise...critical
for understanding the founding of America and for insuring the
future strength of America as 'One Nation Under God.'"*

Agape Press

What sets the national bestseller *George Washington's Sacred Fire* apart from all previous works on this man for the ages, is the exhaustive fifteen years of Dr. Peter Lillback's research, revealing a unique icon driven by the highest of ideals. Only do George Washington's own writings, journals, letters, manuscripts, and those of his closest family and confidants reveal the truth of this awe-inspiring role model for all generations.

Dr. Lillback paints a picture of a man, who, faced with unprecedented challenges and circumstances, ultimately drew upon his persistent qualities of character - honesty, justice, equity, perseverance, piety, forgiveness, humility, and servant leadership, to become one of the most revered figures in world history.

George Washington set the cornerstone for what would become one of the most prosperous, free nations in the history of civilization. Through this book, Dr. Lillback, assisted by Jerry Newcombe, reveals to the reader a newly inspirational image of General and President George Washington.

 PROVIDENCE FORUM PRESS

# Other Literature by Peter A. Lillback

available at www.ProvidenceForum.org

### PROCLAIM LIBERTY...
### A BROKEN BELL RINGS FREEDOM TO THE WORLD

Dr. Lillback has written this 122-page book in commemoration of the 300th anniversary of religious liberty in America. It is the exciting story of America's beloved Liberty Bell—but more than that, it is the story of America's experience of religious and civil liberty—blessings which began over 300 years ago with William Penn's Charter of Privileges. Written in a narrative form, this book explains how the Liberty Bell has become the worldwide symbol of mankind's aspiration for freedom from the tyranny of repressive governments. As Americans once again fly the flag with pride and sing God Bless America with inspiration, *Proclaim Liberty* will help every patriot, from school children to scholars, understand why the United States was intended to be and is still the "land of the free and the home of the brave."

### LESSONS ON LIBERTY: A PRIMER FOR YOUNG PATRIOTS
*(to be released in 2008)*

Designed for all ages and packed with colorful illustrations, this entertaining and educational hardcover book uses a simple alphabet poem to guide the reader through the fundamental principles of American liberty. Incorporating early nineteenth century dictionary definitions and enhanced graphics, Bible quotations and *Poor Richard's Almanack*, this engaging book adds powerful historic quotes, surprising facts, and truths about our nation's founding to excite young and old about our country—this beacon of liberty for the world. Included also are activity pages to further teach young scholars with a hands-on approach—perforated for easy tear-out, these pages may be reproduced on a copier for group use. James Madison once declared, "*The diffusion of knowledge is the only guardian of true liberty*." Whether in your family, or in a public, Christian or home school setting, please join us in striving to preserve our unparalleled heritage of freedom for future generations by introducing them to these timeless truths.

## FREEDOM'S HOLY LIGHT...
## WITH A FIRM RELIANCE ON DIVINE PROVIDENCE

The flagship publication of The Providence Forum, this easy to read, thirty-five-page booklet recaps America's Judeo-Christian heritage in the foundations and ongoing development of our nation. It presents the stories of the very first covenants of the colonies, leading to and including the Declaration of Independence, The Constitution, The Great Seal of the United States, our flag, the Pledge of Allegiance, our national motto and more. *Freedom's Holy Light* has been distributed coast to coast by individuals, at political and community leadership conferences, religious and homeschool networks, radio stations, Christian schools, and bookstores. *Freedom's Holy Light* is endorsed by, among others, Dr. John DiIulio, former Director of the White House Office of Faith-based and Community Initiatives, US Congressman Joe Pitts, Anthony Cardinal Bevilacqua, and Rabbi Daniel Lapin. This book is as entertaining as it is educational, illuminating the intersection of our Judeo-Christian faith, national history and government. The success of America is still dependent upon what our founders described as a "firm reliance on Divine Providence."

## A TOUR OF THE DOLLAR BILL

One of the most profound tools of influence in our society, indeed in the world, is the almighty American dollar. Remarkably, the one-dollar bill has a story to tell about the history and founding principles of our nation, the men that have steered her course since, and our historic symbols and institutions. It reveals the distinctive principles of America, as determined by our founders. The dollar bill explains the founding faith and values of our nation in various ways, including outlining seven essential moral virtues and recognizing the role of Providence in the formation of our nation. Based on Dr. Lillback's renowned presentation seen around the world, Providence Forum Press designed a careful, but non-exact, replica of the one dollar bill with a written "tour" of America's history as told by Dr. Lillback and the dollar itself. Sadly, people are largely ignorant of the history they handle on a daily basis. This entertaining and educational tool fits in any wallet, just as the authentic dollar does, and can be used in many ways to spread the much forgotten history of America's providential founding.

For these and other unique items and resources, please visit
www.ProvidenceForum.org

# NOTES

# NOTES